Bringing Y

Values Out to Play

A Playbook on Company Values

DEBRA COREY

Table of Contents

Foreword

Debra and I first met in London, August 2015. I was CEO at Reward Gateway, the HR Tech Company, Debra had just completed a stint as Global Reward Director at Page Group and was about to publish her first book: "Effective HR Communication".

We were at the Engagement Excellence conference in London. Debra was third up on the agenda with a presentation titled "How to Communicate with Impact" and I was in the audience. I had no idea who she was and the presentation title sounded pretty routine. But the RG sales team had recommended her to speak and were giddy with excitement to see her on stage. I wondered what they knew that I didn't.

Within minutes of her walking on stage, I knew two things. Firstly, the sales team had unearthed an absolute treasure. Secondly, I absolutely had to hire her.

Bursting with energy, Debra owned the stage and electrified the room. She educated, inspired and joked with the audience of several hundred HR leaders. I've met a lot of conference speakers in my time and there are few who have Debra's ability to connect so quickly and so deeply from that stage. We met for lunch the following Wednesday and two months later she joined my executive team.

Having a Group Reward Director of Debra's experience and capability was complete overkill for my 400-person company – in previous roles she had looked after up to 200,000 people. But I wanted her to revolutionize our reward and benefit structures in just one day a week and spend the other four days working with clients and partnering with me in writing a book on employee engagement together. I wanted her to help me spread the message that good work environments can lead to great business results and develop our increasing knowledge and understanding of what makes great company cultures work.

For the next 3 years, we worked tirelessly together, side by side. Between us, we've visited hundreds of companies in dozens of countries. We listened, analysed, mapped, discussed and debated hundreds of company cultures. We've seen companies from every sector you can imagine and at every stage of growth. The smallest client we've worked with had 25 staff, the largest over 100,000.

Debra is one of the most engaging, warm and generous people you will ever meet. And this means people really open up to her. So, from those hundreds of client meetings, she got to learn all the gossip – all the ups and downs of what went on, all the things that never get written in the news release or on the intranet.

Her work with clients over these last four years has allowed her to develop from an HR Director, specialising in Reward, to one of the most experienced and knowledgeable practitioners in company culture and employee engagement that we have.

Debra is also a wonderful writer. I read her first book, "Effective HR Communications" as a pre-publication draft on a flight from Australia to Hong Kong. Even though I was tired when I boarded the plane, I never got to sleep. The book had me smiling from the first page and I couldn't put it down. Quite something for a book about HR communications!

So yes, Debra is a consultant, yes, she's a world-leading expert, yes, she's a C-suite level corporate practitioner. But she's not dry or staid, instead, she is warm, funny, humble and incredibly practically minded.

The data on employee engagement is stark – depending on where you live, around 60-70% of people are disengaged at work. Avoiding complex definitions, let's say it like this: About 3 in 4 employees arrive at work thinking primarily about what time they can go home. Having strong and wisely chosen internal values that are deeply embedded in processes, procedures – the very fabric of an organisation is a key part of building a culture of high engagement. Debra and I learned that whilst writing our last book, *Build it*, together.

When researching *Build it*, we saw first-hand how companies with the best culture had a really strong sense of who they were and how their people should behave – they had effective values. That's why this book is needed and as you can see from the disengagement statistics, it is needed urgently.

Importantly, this is not a book that will teach you complex models that you'll never get to implement. It's not a book that will bamboozle you with long words or strange concepts. And it's not a book that will gather dust on the shelf.

Instead, it's a book packed with practical tips and actionable examples. There are other books on company values that might tell you how to design them, but this book will tell you how to design, implement, polish and perfect them, doing so in Debra's rebellious, but still practical way.

It will educate you on what is possible, equip you with tools to make the process possible and it will inspire you as to what is possible.

It's been an honor working with Debra these last 4 years and I've been privileged to have seen this book in some of its early forms. I hope you enjoy reading this book as much as I have. And I hope most of all, you get to use it to make real, positive change in your own organization.

Glenn Elliott,
Author, Founder and Former CEO at Reward Gateway
Berlin, October 2019

"You can't stop the future. You can't rewind the past. The only way to learn the secret . . . is to press play."

– Jay Asher, *Thirteen Reasons Why*

Introduction

"Houston, we have a problem" is probably the most famous sentence ever spoken in space, coming from the radio communications between the Apollo 13 crew and the NASA mission control center. I'd like to borrow this powerful phrase, because **we, too, have a problem**!

The problem is that although the majority of companies have published values, data from Gallup shows that only 27 percent of employees strongly believe in them, and only 23 percent of employees strongly agree they can apply their organization's values to their work. That's three out of four employees who don't believe in and/or don't use their company values as they go about their work, taking actions and making decisions that ultimately impact on the success of their company.

So why is this a problem? Why should it matter that values are not play- ing a role in how employees are working? To answer this, let's go back to the Apollo 13 story, where the problem they faced was returning their astronauts safely to Earth after an oxygen tank exploded. They overcame horrific challenges to safely return their astronauts, achieving this happy ending because everyone at NASA worked together, doing so by not only understanding their values but applying them in every decision and action they made.

In this real-life situation, their values of being *team-oriented*: coming together to solve complex issues, being *agile*: working in ambiguous environments, and being *resilient*: not giving up, were ultimately the difference between life and death for their three astronauts! And, by the way, I'm absolutely confident that the values weren't listed in a manual or hung up on the walls of the spacecraft – instead, they were intrinsic to each and every employee at NASA, in space and on the ground!

But surely this only happens in space travel; values can't have such an important role to play in the "normal" business world. Wrong! Jim Collins and Jerry Porras conducted an extensive six-year research project which found that visionary and exceptional companies were all guided by a core ideology, core values and a sense of purpose that are beyond just making money. In *Built to Last,* they write that "A deeply held core ideology gives a company both a strong sense of identity and thread of continuity that holds the organization together." They believed so much in the importance of values, that they are one of the six "timeline fundamentals" suggested to organizations in order to build their own visionary and successful company.

So, if values are strategic tools required of businesses, what can we do to *make* our employees understand and apply them? The answer is to start by admitting that the problem is actually not with our employees, but with us! The Gallup data clearly shows that the majority of companies:

1. **Don't have the "right" values**, ones that truly describe and guide their workforce to achieve their mission, helping them understand what behaviors are to be applied in good times and in bad.

2. **Don't fully operationalize our values**, embedding and weaving them into everything they do, being so much a part of how they operate that even if they were nowhere in sight, their employees would know, believe in, and live them in their behaviors and actions.

> *"If you're not going to take the time to translate values from ideals to behaviors—if you're not going to teach people the skills they need to show up in a way that's aligned with those values and then create a culture in which you hold one another accountable for staying aligned with the values— it's better not to profess any values at all. They become a joke. A cat poster. Total BS."*
>
> – Brené Brown, researcher and author, *Dare to Lead*

But all is not lost, for there are ways to overcome these problems. Over my 20 plus years as a Human Resources Leader and now as a writer, speaker and consultant, I've worked at, or have met companies who are getting it right. They're changing the statistics at their company and achieving their mission and purpose through their people applying and living their values.

And this is exactly why I've written this book, to share the tips, tools and stories I've lived, learned or collected from others through my research and consulting, so that every company can benefit from the power of values, using them as an integral part of their wider engagement strategy. Do this, and you'll have an engaged workforce that uses your strategic values to guide them to achieve your mission . . . even if you have a challenge like they did on Apollo 13!

Getting Started

Before you begin your values "journey", which is a term I'll use throughout the book to signify that you'll be taking many small and big steps to get to your destination, let me share a few things about the book to help you and get you on your way:

● **You don't have to read the book front to back.**

Although the order of the chapters is somewhat sequential, you certainly don't need to follow them in numerical order. Depending on where you are in your values journey and processes, feel free to dip into chapters (and plays) at different times and for different reasons. In fact, I hope you use it this way to refer to and inspire you not just once, but whenever the need may arise.

● **Use the book as a playbook.**

This book is not a textbook, it is not a reference book, it is a playbook.

This means that just as a sports playbook includes strategies and approaches to get things done, this book is packed with a variety of approaches, techniques and tips to help you get things done. Use it like a playbook – scribble in it, draw in it, rip pages out of it, have fun with it!

- **Be inspired by the plays.**

  This book, like my last book, is jam-packed with stories, or what I call plays. They are intended to inspire and inform you by sharing how other companies have discovered, embedded and live their values. I absolutely loved interviewing all of the companies, and I'm certain you'll love reading the plays, walking away with tons of ideas.

- **Go out and play with your values.**

  The title of this book, and the concept of "playing with your values" came to me partly because of my approach to sharing stories through my plays, and partly through reading Nikki Gatenby's book, *Superengaged*, where she has a section header saying "Bring your values out to play". This concept resonates with me, and hopefully with you, for playing is such a powerful and effective way to learn and grow. If we can bring this into the workplace when it comes to our values, think of the magic that will happen!

As Lao Tzu, a Chinese philosopher and writer, once said, "A journey of a thousand miles begins with a single step." So, with that being said, let's take our first step together!

CHAPTER 1

The power of values

CHAPTER OBJECTIVES

In this chapter, we'll cover:

- What values are and how they can be defined.
- Why values are valuable.

Introduction

In this chapter, I'll be answering two key questions – what are values, and why are they so important and so darn powerful? I'm confident that many, if not all of you, already know the answers to these questions, but I wanted to quickly cover them for two reasons:

1. So that we all are on "the same page" on these basic but important concepts.

2. So that when you're asked these questions from business leaders or from your workforce, you'll have something you can cut and paste to do so – my gift to you!

What are values?

Let's start from the beginning by answering the question, what are values? Put simply, values are a set of words and explanatory sentences or paragraphs that state or suggest behaviors that the company has in some way decided are valuable, unique and important to them.

Or as Jim Collins and Jerry Porras say in their book, *Built to Last*, values are "the organization's essential and enduring tenets – a small set of time-liness guiding principles that require no external justification; they have *intrinsic* value and are important to those inside the organization."

Why are values . . . valuable?

To answer the question of why values are valuable, let me start by once again referencing Jim Collins and Jerry Porras, and the research they did over a six-year period and wrote about in their book, *Built to Last*. They show that the biggest and most successful, durable and sustainable companies all had a single thing in common that transcended their CEO, their products and even their markets, which was a strongly embedded sense of who they were, which comes from their purpose and their values.

Building on from this, here are four other reasons I've seen (and felt) as to why values can and should be important to your organization:

1. **They define who you are.**

    Values define who you are as a business, what you stand for (and against), and what you are willing to fight for. This is important because it tells potential and existing employees and customers what you believe in and how you'll behave, clearly defining this upfront in a meaningful way. And in this competitive world, the better we can do this through our values, the better chance we have of standing out from our competitors and attracting and retaining talent and customers.

2. **They guide decisions and actions**.

Values act as guidelines, guiding principles, and/or guideposts to your employees, helping them make everyday operational and strategic decisions, even when leaders are not around. When used properly, employees use them to ask questions such as, "what do my values say about this?" and "how can my values help me choose a path and make a decision?" This is important at all times, but especially in bad or challenging ones, where values provide the focus and guidance we need to persevere.

> *"Values are needed as principles that guide our behavior while we're scaling the mountain we set to climb."*
> **– Ken Blanchard and Garry Ridge,** *Helping People Win at Work.*

A great example of an employee using their values "on the spot" to guide decision-making was told to me by Troels Wendelbo, Senior HR Director at LEGO Group.

The story took place at a LEGO Group store in London, England, when a customer came in looking for a LEGO set for his wedding cake. He told the member of staff that although he could find a set with a bride and a groom, he couldn't find one with two grooms, which was necessary since his was a same-sex wedding. The employee replied by taking two ready-made sets and built a new set for the customer, one with two grooms, and charged him the same price. By doing this, the employee lived pretty much all of the values and created a wonderful experience for the customer (and everyone attending the wedding).

3. **Values *fuel your workforce*.**

Values give employees the energy and passion to not only make decisions but to get things done. To bring this point to life, let's go back to the Apollo 13 story shared in the Introduction, which involved dealing with a life-threatening challenge. Their values of being agile and resilient were not only used to drive their decision-making, but to fuel a commitment to seeing things through to the end, even when their ideas and decisions didn't work and they had to try other options. This passion, this energy, is so critical in the business world, and when being led by values, it ensures that it's being done in the right way and in the right direction.

Values help prepare us for moments that we don't even know are coming, giving us energy we no longer have (or think we have) to get us to our destination.

4. **They contribute to driving employee engagement.**

As shown in the Engagement Bridge™ model created and shared in my book, *Build it: The Rebel Playbook for Employee Engagement*, values along with purpose and mission are an integral part of employee engagement. And, as studies have shown, engagement improves productivity, customer and employee retention, and profit to name a few.

> Companies with high engagement have 17 percent higher productivity, 20 percent higher sales, and 21 percent higher profitability – Gallup study.

TIPS TO PLAY WITH

✪ Remember what you're trying to achieve

Keep in mind throughout your values journey, that as Simon Sinek says, "it all starts with why." Make sure that you create your own version of the "why" for your values based on what your business needs, your workforce needs, and what you are trying to achieve through your purpose, mission and values. Use this throughout your journey as you focus on your target, going back from time to time to make sure that you're on course to achieve your objectives.

✪ Don't keep it to yourself

If you want your leaders and your workforce to truly embrace your values, you'll need to share with them the "why". Explain to them why the company has the values and why they're important to the business and to them personally. Quoting Simon Sinek again, your employees "don't buy what you do but why you do it".

CHAPTER 2

Discovering your values

CHAPTER OBJECTIVES

In this chapter, we'll cover:

● Why you should discover and not design your values.
● How you can discover your values through six steps.

Introduction

Now that we've explored the "why", let's swiftly move on to the next phase of the journey, which is "discovering" your values. If you have values already, please don't skip this chapter, but instead, use it as a way to check that what you have is truly meeting your needs. If you don't have them yet, use this chapter as a way to help you as you begin your journey, setting your employees and business up for success by discovering values that are not just words, but are strategic and effective business and engagement tools.

Company values can have a dramatic effect on your organization, so make sure they are the right ones. It takes time, but it is hugely valuable.

Discovery versus design

In *Built to Last,* they say that "you do not create or set values; instead you discover them." When I read this for the first time, a light bulb went off in my head, being one of those true aha moments. I thought to myself, no wonder so many companies get it wrong when it comes to values. We're trying to design them from scratch instead of looking from within, going on a journey of self-discovery to uncover what makes us special and what makes us who we are.

The journey to discover our true company values involves looking at what we already *say*, what we already *do*, what we already *believe*, and what we want and need to *protect*.

This way of thinking aligns with a method of teaching called "discovery learning", that encourages learners to build on their past experiences and knowledge, using their intuition, imagination and creativity to look for new information to discover facts, correlations and new truths. The benefits of this method of learning, as well as the discovery approach to values-creation, are:

1. It **delivers the best solutions** as the process leverages existing knowledge and expertise of your employees.

2. It **improves buy-in** as employees have a much more active role in the process.

3. It **improves retention** of the information as employees are not just learning but are understanding and participating.

4. And finally, you have a much better chance that employees will **believe in their values**. And, since according to a Gallup study[1], only 1 in 4 employees in the U.S. say that they believe in their company values, this is certainly something that needs to be improved.

1   Taken from Gallup Business Journal – September 13, 2016.

7 steps to discover your values

For the remainder of this chapter, I'll be sharing with you the following seven steps which you can use to help discover your values. These steps can be followed if you're discovering values for the first time, for a refresh, or if you're reading this book and want to do a check of the effectiveness of your values.

1. Start planning
2. Stick them on the walls
3. Invite them to the table
4. Test them out
5. Select the winners
6. Define them with behaviours
7. Set them free

Step 1: Start planning

The first step in the discovery process is the planning, which is all about taking a step back and thinking through exactly how you'll get things done. This is important because it forces you to think things through before you begin your journey, making sure that once you begin you don't have to turn around or start over because you've forgotten or have gotten something wrong.

Determine who should join you on the journey

One of the most important questions you'll have to answer before embarking on your journey is, "who should be involved when we discover our values?" Do I use a *top-down* approach, meaning it comes from the top leaders of my company, or a *bottom-up* approach, meaning it comes from my workforce, or a combination or version of these two approaches?

Great question, and something that needs to be decided upfront as it will have a huge impact on the outcome. Unfortunately, there is no perfect answer to this question, as it will depend on your company, your culture, your workforce, your timing, and even what else is happening at your company.

That being said, my "go-to" approach has always been some version of a bottom-up approach. By involving my employees, I've been able to achieve the four benefits which I listed previously in this chapter – delivering the best solution, improving buy-in, improving retention, and having values that are believed in.

> 39% of employees surveyed wished they had more involvement in contributing to the company's vision and values – Rungway study

There are, however, times when a bottom-up approach will not work or is not possible. An example comes from an interview I had with Valor Hospitality. They explained that although they wanted employees to be involved in the journey and the process, they used a top-down approach because they were going through a great deal of change, so they didn't have the people or time to use this approach. This worked for them at this time and in this situation.

> My own research shows that 55 percent of companies had employees involved in discovering their values, 25 percent did not, and 20 percent did not know.

The most important thing I've learned over the years when it comes to what approach to use and who to include, is to ask yourself the question, "who will help me discover and uncover the best values for my company?" The last thing you want to do is get to the end of the process and realize that you don't have what you need to complete the task, or that you only have one or two perspectives.

Think carefully about who you will invite to be a part of your values journey, for getting it wrong will certainly delay or derail your journey.

Determine who will be on your lead team

Just as important as deciding who will join you on your journey to discover your values, is deciding who will be on your "lead" team. What I mean by this is, who will make up a smaller project team to help you navigate throughout the journey and help you make the important decision.

When selecting your team, it's important to include individuals from different functions, levels and demographics. This does two things: it ensures you have a mix of ideas and perspectives, and it gives additional credibility to the project.

Also key, is having senior-level involvement in your lead team. By including them throughout the journey, you get their buy-in and their much-needed support and ability to influence. It also shows your workforce that your values are a business tool and not merely a Human Resources tool.

Determine the "right" time to go on the journey

Another important question to ask upfront is the question about timing, so when is it the "right" time to discover your values, either for the first time or for a subsequent time?

Let's tackle the first part of the question, which is discovering values for the first time. I'm a big believer in having values sooner rather than later. And the reason is quite simple – if you have a tool, especially such a powerful tool as values, why wait to pull it out of your toolkit?

Many start-ups I've spoken to have told me that they're too busy at the beginning to discover their values. They need to focus on getting their business up and running, and besides, if they only have a few employees, then why do they need values when everyone knows what we're doing anyway? But do they? If you aren't clear on what your values are upfront, you're making a huge assumption and putting your company at risk of going in the wrong direction or getting there using different paths.

Before you say you're too busy or you don't need values, ask yourself, can I live with the risk of not having them?

Let's move on to the second part of the question, which is, when is it right to change my values? In a perfect world, you'd discover and put your values in place once, and then leave them alone to be lived over and over again. However, as we all know, we don't live in a perfect world, so in some situations, you may find yourself in a place where you need to change one or more of your values.

It is important to treat these situations with caution, only doing so if it is entirely necessary. Think of it like the name of your child or pet; how confusing would it be to them if you all of a sudden change their name? And with values, it's more than just a name or a word, but a way of being or living, so don't upset "the apple cart", as the expression goes, unless you believe that by doing so it will deliver more good than bad.

My own research shows that about half of the companies have either changed their values or their behaviors at least once, 27 percent have always had the same values in place, and the other 18 percent did not know.

Here are a few situations when you may consider changing your values:

- **Your business and your purpose or mission has changed**.
  In this situation, you realize that your current values will hold you back or even prevent you from meeting your new objectives.

- **A value no longer drives the right behaviors**.
  In this situation, you find that your value, or the words used to describe the value, no longer deliver the behaviors required from your workforce.

- **You no longer need a value.**
  In this situation, you find that a value is no longer needed because it's either become a part of another value, or you realize that it no longer makes sense.

For example, let's say you finish reading this book, go through the checklist, and find that a value doesn't make it through the decision-making filter. Don't be afraid to remove a value if you feel it is not doing what it needs to, but be certain that you have a clear and compelling story for your workforce. And sorry, it can't be "because Debra told me to".

When Nav, a U.S. FinTech company, was a start-up, they didn't have formal company values. Rather, the company had a culture that encouraged employees to "Be a hero", which talked about stepping up and fixing a problem or a situation. According to Levi King, CEO & Co-Founder, it worked well in the early years, however as they grew, it began to hurt the business as teamwork and collaboration became more important. The "Be a hero" mantra was replaced with the value of "indivisible", which talks about working hard together with intellectual honesty, wisdom and real-time communication, all while having each other's backs.

Read the full play in Chapter 6

The outcome of this step is to have mapped out how, when and with whom you'll go on your journey. Think of it as packing your bags before you set off.

Step 2: Stick them on the walls

This is where the discovery and the fun begin, for in this step you will physically or figuratively put all of your ideas for values up on the walls. You can go about doing this in many ways, whether it's conducting surveys, holding focus groups, or a combination of both (my personal preference).

But as fun as this step is, I know from experience that at first, it may seem like an ominous task, as you don't know where to begin or how to get this important information. The key is to be absolutely clear as to what you are looking for, since as the expression goes, "garbage in, garbage out".

Here are two ways to achieve this and to set expectations:

1. Make sure that everyone understands the "**why**", so why your business needs values – feel free to share the four reasons that appear in Chapter 1.

2. Make sure that everyone understands the "**what**", so what your values will be used for so that they are clear as to how this will impact them personally as well as the company.

A helpful way of explaining this, and a way that many companies use, comes from *Built to Last.* "Imagine you've been asked to recreate the very best attributes of your organization on another planet," he says, "but you only have seats on the rocket ship for five to seven people. Who would you choose?" It is this group – the famous Mars Group – that they say should be entrusted with establishing the values of your organization down here on Earth.

Now, let me say that as much as I love the "Mars Group" concept, I've found that for many, they need a bit more direction and clarity to help determine who will be the values "passengers." So, I start with the Mars concept, and then go into further detail by sharing the following four questions, which serve as a filter to help decide which values go up on the wall.

1. Are they servants to my purpose or mission?

The first question you should ask is, which values will help you be **servants** to your purpose or mission? Which will support, align and drive your company's purpose or mission forward, keeping you focused on what your business is trying to achieve?

One of my favorite Olympic stories brings this concept to life, and is written about in the book *Will it Make the Boat Go Faster* by Harriet Beveridge and Ben Hunt-Davis. In it, they tell the story of how the British Olympic rowing team in 2000 used one single question, "Will it make the boat go faster?" to help them win a gold medal.

What I love about this story is that the British team were the underdogs (who doesn't love an underdog, right?). In fact, if you listen to the commentator, you'll hear that up until the very end of the race he expected them to crash and burn, and to lose the lead they'd maintained throughout the race. But, driven by their uncompromising focus on their mission of winning a gold through their commitment to their one question, they surprised the world and won. If, in the business world, we adopt this approach of using our values as a way to stay true to our purpose and mission, using them to focus us in the right direction, then I strongly believe our workforce and businesses will perform and win in the competitive world we operate in.

> **Your values are darts which need to hit a target, your mission.**
>
> Picture your company's mission or purpose as the target at the center of a dartboard. Now picture your values as your darts. When you throw them, do they hit the target or somewhere else? If they don't hit the target, then you should be questioning whether they are true values, as they aren't helping you achieve your mission.

2. Are they specific to my company?

Another question to ask is, which values will be specific to my company? I already said that they need to be specific to your purpose and mission, but this isn't enough as you need to have values that specifically relate to, and are meaningful to, your culture and to your way of working, helping you say and do things in your own way. As Patrick Lencioni said in an article in the Harvard Business Review, "Cookie-cutter values don't set a company apart from competitors; they make it fade into the crowd." In addition to this, if you have values that are not specific to your company, employees will see them as just another thing that HR 'did to them'!

"In a volatile, uncertain, complex and ambiguous world, where the only constant is change, authenticity is key. It's not about 'best practice' and copying others, it's about 'fit for purpose', getting right underneath what you are as an organization, what you want to be, and then making everything you say and do true to you."

– Jane Sunley, Chairman and Founder of Purple Cubed

To illustrate this point, here are eight examples of companies I interviewed for this book who designed their own specific values that have their root in the concept of **innovation**:

Atlassian	C Space	giffgaff	Missguided
Be the change you seek.	Do what scares you.	Be curious: We talk. We listen. We challenge. We find a better way.	Dream big: Use ideas and innovation to lead the way.

Nav	Otsuka	Reward Gateway	Zappos
Unruly: Ruthlessly creative in challenging the status quo while never accepting roadblocks.	Creativity: We embrace unconventional thinking and welcome innovative solutions.	Push the boundaries.	Be adventurous, creative and open-minded.

When Australian telecoms company, Vocus Communications, went through a merger and increased its workforce 10-fold, the company realized it needed to define a new identity by updating company values to ones that worked for all employees, regardless of which business they came from. It also opened up the opportunity to create new values that "tied people together and gave them a common language" according to Denise Hanlon, former HR Director.

An example is the value of not being a "d!@khead," which gives employees a commonly acceptable word for calling each other out when they're not behaving according to the values. "We've created values that are more than words; they have their own energy; they are a call to action. They make a massive difference to the way we treat our customers and our employees. In a company created from many other companies over time, they are our True North," says Hanlon.

3. Can (and will) they be lived and acted on?

The next question, or rather point to make, is that once values are put in place there will be an expectation that they will be lived and acted on. This means that both the business and employees will be expected to behave and make decisions based on these, so make sure that they are not only liveable, but by acting on them it will drive the right behaviors.

Be absolutely clear about this upfront so that when ideas and values start to fill the wall, participants understand the consequences of each and every value. And remember, values aren't just for good days, but for rainy ones, for ones when you need to easily and swiftly move from Plan A to Plan B. Effective values drive actions at all levels and at all times.

> *"Many companies have core values, but they don't really commit to them. They usually sound more like something you'd read in a press release. We believe that it's really important to come up with core values that you can commit to. And by commit, we mean that you're willing to hire and fire based on them. If you're willing to do that, then you're well on your way to building a company culture that is in line with the brand you want to build."*
>
> **– Tony Hsieh, CEO, Zappos, from *Delivering Happiness***

Standard practice in the travel industry, and a way that travel companies make money, is for companies to keep the customer's deposit if the customer cancels a trip. However, a group of G Adventure employees asked whether that was taking advantage of people's misfortune, pointing out that it went against their value of "doing the right thing."

Poon Tip, G Adventure's Founder and CEO, and the leadership team decided the employees were right, and came up with the revolutionary idea of a lifetime deposit, meaning a customer doesn't lose a deposit but can apply it toward a new trip, give it to someone else or donate it to G Adventure's charity.

This is a great example of living company values, with them clearly showing both customers and employees who they are, helping employees and the business get to the next level.

A values-led business uses its values as an hourly and daily tool for problem-solving and decision-making. They're ever-present, not being something that is brought out only when it's convenient or opportunistic.

4. Can (and will) they take us to a new planet?

The next question is about the future and looks at which values you need to take you to a new "planet", achieving your future goals and objectives. In Patrick Lencioni's book, *The Advantage,* he calls these *aspirational values*, saying that "They are neither natural nor inherent, which is why they must be purposefully inserted into the culture."

Too often, we focus on the here and now in the values exercise, so the more you can make this point about the future, the better chance you have at getting there safely, and, at the same time, not having to revisit your values again.

The outcome of this step is to have collected as many ideas and potential values as possible that answer the four questions listed at the start of this step. Picture a room filled with quality-written Post-it notes, and that's what success looks like!

Step 3: Invite them to the table

If step two is where the fun begins, step three is where the hard work begins. And that's because, at the end of step two, you have a huge, if slightly unmanageable, list of values up on the wall.

But that's fine, for this is where you bring in your lovely project team, having them help you turn this chaos into a masterpiece. And just like with the last step, the first thing to do is to set expectations. Be clear that the purpose and desired outcome is to end up with a list of values that *deserve a seat at the table.* And like a table, there are only so many seats around it, so you'll need to have those difficult (but lively) discussions in order to decide which ones are, and which ones are not, seat-worthy.

Your company values should be ones that you just can't walk away from as they are so critical to the life, health and success of your business.

One approach for helping you narrow down and fine-tune your list of values is by using the "keep, kill, and combine" process. For each value, go back and decide which of these three actions to take:

● **Keep: *put a tick next to these***

These are the values that tick all, if not most, of the questions in step one. These are the ones that you absolutely cannot walk away from as they are at the heart and core of who you are and what you want to be.

● **Kill: *draw a line through these***

These are the values that either don't tick any of the question boxes, or if they tick one, they are in conflict with the others, e.g. could cause problems to these.

They could also be what Patrick Lencioni, in his book *The Advantage,* calls permission-to-play values, which he describes as being "the minimum behavioral standards that are required in an organization". Values often seen in this category are those such as trust, integrity and ethics. Now don't get me wrong, these are absolutely essential to have at any company; in fact, they are like the air that we breathe. But my question and challenge is – should they be standalone values? Or instead, should they be woven into your values, thus making them an integral and natural part of how you run your business and how employees behave?

For example, if you believe that trust should be one of your values, ask yourself why? What does trust really mean and why do we need it to make our company great? Is it trust in how you work together, in how you communicate with each other, or in how you respect each other? Pinpoint the behaviors related to trust that you need to see, and then weave these into your values that truly deserve a seat at the table.

● **Combine: *circle these***

These are the values that are similar to one another, so could be combined to have a better overall impact. Look for themes amongst these, so that you can narrow them down and cluster them together.

The outcome of this step is to have a manageable list that you can take forward to the next step. How you define manageable is up to you, but the focus at this stage should be less about the number of values and more about the quality of values. Take forward those that you can easily and readily explain and defend – that is the key.

Step 4: Test them out

Great; you now have a list of what could be your values. At this point, you probably want to tick the box to say that you're finished, but alas, there is still work to be done. During this step, you'll need to throw the values you've come up with in the previous step up against the wall, seeing if they "stick" by checking if and how they resonate with your workforce.

> *"The real voyage of discovery consists not in seeking new land-scapes, but in having new eyes."*
>
> **– Marcel Proust**

It's important to go through this process with both your leaders and the rest of your workforce, as they both have different needs and different perspectives.

- **For leaders**, you'll need to test that the values are ones that will drive the business strategy, and at the same time, drive the right behaviors. They need to ask themselves, will they help me hire the right people – recognize the right behaviors – manage performance – and, when things get tough, help or hinder decision-making? Will they help me be a better leader? And finally, will I be able to embrace and role-model them?

- **For your workforce**, you'll need to test that they speak to your employees in a way that they help them understand them, as well as understand what is expected of them. Try to uncover whether they will create an emotional connection, getting your workforce excited and behind them.

By the way, to thoroughly test your draft values, you need to not just evaluate *what they say* when sharing feedback, but *how they say it*. Look out for any and every cue, so that you can capture genuine reactions and feelings.

Another thing to keep in mind is that, as with anything, you are not going to please everyone. A value may be loved by the majority of those you've gone to, but hated by others. Your job is to consider all input, but then to make decisions that are right for your business and your overall work-

> At Zappos, they had hundreds of ideas for values come in from their workforce, which they then dwindled down to 37. They then spent the good part of a year brainstorming and working together to come up with their final ten values.
>
> It was very much an iterative and collaborative process, going back and forth and testing values with their employees over and over again. "If your employees are expected to live them, they need to be a part of developing them," says Maritza Lewis, Employee Engagement Manager. Read the full play in Chapter 6

force, explaining why you've made these decisions.

The result of this step is that you feel confident that you have *stress-tested* your draft values, and have all the feedback and input you need to go to the next step.

Step 5: Select the winners

Not that you've completed the discovery steps, it's time to get down to work and select your winners, the values that have safely made it through the previous four steps, showing that they have what it takes to *win the competition*.

"Creativity is all about subtraction, which is why we challenged each and every value put forward, throwing them all in a funnel, and only having those that defined what made us unique end up in our final four values."

– Alastair Gill, People Partner at giffgaff.

The questions to address during this step are:

How many values should we have?

I'm often asked, how many values should I have? Is there a "magic" or a "perfect" number? Personally, I'd answer this question yes ... and no. And that's because it depends on your company, your workforce, your culture, and what you need your values to do for your business.

I'm a big believer in the expression "less is more" when it comes to life,

> My own research shows that the number of values ranged from two to ten. The most common responses were: 37.5% had five values, 21% had four values, and 18.5% had three values.

and also when it comes to your values. And for this reason, I'd suggest that if more than five values have made it through to this step, that you give them one more round of review, making sure that they all deserve to be winners. Since they'll all need to be remembered and lived by your workforce, you want to be 100 percent sure that they are worth the extra effort.

Let me pause for a moment and say that this does not mean that you should never have more than five values. I've heard this said before, and I don't agree with it. And the reason is that each company is different, having different business needs, cultures and workforces, so in all cases, five values may just not be able to address these differences. The key is to not focus on the 'magic number', but to focus on making sure that each and every value you end up with is a 'winner'. And if you want proof of having ten values that are truly winners, just check out Zappos's ten fantastic values in their play in Chapter 6.

An example of a company having more than five values that are all 'winners' is Southwest Airlines. They do something unique by having a multi-level approach to values, defining expectations through their values as employees progress upward through the organization.

The first level is for all employees and includes their three values of Warrior Spirit, Servant's Heart and Fun-LUVing Attitude. The second level is for all leaders, and includes Develop People, Build Great Teams and Thinking Strategically. The third level is additional expectations for all senior leaders, and includes Demonstrate Capacity, Communicate Effectively and Be Knowledgeable. By setting specific expectations at leadership levels, it believes the company better supports employees who, in turn, better support customers – thus providing a terrific customer experience.

If you allow people to be individuals, then you don't create an army of 'everyone speaks the same' robots. You get a system where people can be honest about which values they love and do without thinking, and which they respect but they have to make a conscious effort with."

– Glenn Elliott, Tech Entrepreneur & Author

How will they work together?

Have you ever read a set of values and thought to yourself, "how in the world do these ever fit or work together?" It's almost like someone took a deck of cards with random values written on them, dropped them to the floor, and whichever ones landed face side up were the ones the company decided to use.

So, if you want your values to work, they need to work together. If they either work against each other or aren't pulled together in one way, employees will start using them as weapons, using one against the other, undermining all that you've created with your values. So, consciously think about this when you are selecting your final values.

One way that WD-40 Company has its values work together is by creating a hierarchy, rank-ordering them based on how they should be lived and how they should be prioritized. By doing this, employees aren't able to cherry-pick which value to use in any given situation. The hierarchical structure provides clarity to guide their decision-making and protect the best interest of the company, the culture, the brands and shareholders.

"We recognize that life is full of conflicts when it comes to living values. Sometimes you can't honor two values at the same time. That's why our values are force-ranked, and our first value, *doing the right thing*, is more important than all others," says Garry Ridge, CEO.

Read full play in Chapter 6

What should we call them?

Throughout the book, you'll notice that I use the term "value". However, let me say that in no way am I saying that you MUST use this term. Yes, it's a commonly accepted term, but I'm a big fan, if you haven't realized already, of being your own company and doing things in your own way. So, call them what you'd like, and by the way, if you do come up with something unique and original, please let me know!

And, to give you some inspiration for doing it your own way, here are examples from companies I interviewed for this book:

- **Dishoom** call their two values *Seva*
- **Impraise** call their six values their *6-pack*
- **Missguided** call their values their *Vibes*
- **Peoplecare** call them their *True Loves*

At Missguided, an online fashion retailer, they call their values "vibes". The reason is that when they did their initial listening groups, which they called "Holla sessions", the language used by employees talked about having good vibes.

"When I looked up the word "vibes" in the dictionary, it talked about a *person's emotional state or the atmosphere of a place as communicated to and felt by others* – which is exactly what we were trying to define and develop through our values," says Glenn Grayson, Internal Communications & Engagement Partner.

Also, as a brand, they've often used the theme of "Good Vibes only" in their external marketing. So, by picking up on the word "vibes", they were able to create alignment and synergy between their internal and external brands. And to take it that one step further, the HR team decided to use "Good Vibes only" as the name for their employee recognition program. That certainly drives the right behaviors and creates a positive feeling.

Read the full play in Chapter 6.

At Dishoom, a restaurant group, they call their values "Seva". The name stems from Dishoom's core belief about humanity, a belief that people are at their happiest and best when they are sharing whole-heartedly of themselves and contributing to the world to the best of their abilities.

"Our view is that it's part of human nature to care about making people happy. We all care about this deeply. We call this Seva. Seva means having a big, warm, open heart. And Seva means wanting to be fantastic – first-class – at everything you do. Seva means we don't just serve people, we take them in and look after them to the very best of our ability – guests and team alike," says Andrew O'Callaghan, Head of People.

Read the full play in Chapter 6.

How can they be truly meaningful?

If your values are truly going to resonate with your workforce, they have to create an immediate and ongoing meaning and emotional connection with them. This is something that you will have reviewed during the testing step, so use this information to make sure that whatever word(s) you use for your final values reflects this.

One final way to make sure you create this meaning is to make sure you've removed any buzzwords or corporate jargon. I often do a final test with my teenage children, testing their reaction and understanding. If they, who have little experience in the corporate world, don't "get it", then there's a good chance my workforce won't.

> More than a quarter (27%) feel that their company's vision or values have too much corporate jargon and one in five (18%) say they don't reflect what the company is actually like – Rungway survey

When C Space, a Customer Agency, discovered and developed their values, they thought carefully about the meaning of each value, asking themselves what behaviors and actions they would drive. An example of this was their value of *I've got this*, which was put in place to "nudge employees to take full ownership of a task or problem that needed solving and discourage passing the buck" said Phil Burgess, Chief People and Operations Officer. Another example is their value of *only accept awesome*, which "was a reminder that the firm had to wow its clients, leave them amazed, not merely satisfied," said Burgess.

Read the full play in Chapter 6.

Let's be honest, how much can busy people remember? This means that you need to use every tool and every trick to make your values memorable so that they . . . will be remembered. One way I've seen work well is through the use of acronyms, thus cueing employees to the individual values through the acronym, and sometimes even giving them a special meaning or identity through the value itself.

When interviewing the companies for this book, I came across some great examples of companies using this effective technique. Here are seven of them:

Radio Flyer	Nav	MOSL	ICC Sydney
FLYER	RULIO	ERIC	ICCS
CarTrawler	**St John**	**Valor Hospitality**	
HOPES	**Ambulance**	PRIDE	
	HEART		

At Purple Cubed, an employee engagement consultancy, they created the acronym AFFIRM IT for their eight values. Here's what Jane Sunley, Chairman and Founder, said about how and why they came up with this:

"When I founded the business with one other person, we sat down and talked about what really mattered to us and how we were going to keep our business true to itself and to us as we grew it. We ended up with eight values, which we knew were far too many; we'd never recommend that amount to a client. However, they were all important, so we came up with our 'AFFIRM IT' acronym so that our future employees would be able to easily recall them. In the 18 years we've been in business, we've only made one change. The second 'I' used to stand for 'Innovation', though it had become an 'overdone word' so we changed it to 'Improve – with originality'. Over the years they've served us well."

Step 6: Define them with behaviors

Fantastic, you've now selected your winning values, congratulations! This is a huge accomplishment, so by all means celebrate, but then very quickly move on to this important next step, which involves defining them. This is where you take your values to the next level, giving them clarity, depth, and what I like to think of as a personality and a voice, or what we commonly call behaviors.

> *"Documented behaviors that all employees KNOW and DO are the pot of gold at the end of the rainbow."*
>
> **– Gregg Lederman, *Engaged!***

This step is so critical, and yet so often overlooked, as companies assume that their employees will magically know exactly what their values mean and start "playing with them". But just like if you handed someone a ball to play with and said they were to jump in and play a game, if you don't give your employees behaviors, they too won't know the 'rules of the game' and how to play with the 'ball', your values. If you don't do this, or if don't do it in a clear and effective way, your values will either be ignored or used in the wrong way. Not something you want for your people or for your business, so it's important to get it right!

If you want your employees to play with your values, you need to give them the 'rules of the game', letting them know exactly what they mean in action. Don't leave it to chance – it's too important.

Make behaviors meaningful

Earlier, I made the point that it's important to discover values that are meaningful to your unique business and to your unique people. Well, the same is important, if not more so, when it comes to defining your behaviors. Since these explain and provide the details on how to behave, make decisions and get work done at your company, careful attention needs to be paid to ensure they are done in a meaningful way so that they drive the right behaviors with your workforce. So as with values, ban all jargon and corporate speak, and work on making these mean something and speak to your workforce so that they drive your business.

One way you can do this is to make sure that the behaviors you create, like your values, *tick all the boxes*. Below, you'll find the four questions listed earlier for discovering your values, along with a few others that will help you get at the core and essence of what your behaviors need to be:

1. Are they servants to my purpose or mission? Will they drive and support my company's purpose or mission, having my employees behave in a way that is aligned with them?	
2. Are they specific to my company? Are they specific to your culture and to your way of working, helping you say and do things in your own way?	
3. Can (and will) they be lived? Can the business and employees behave and make decisions based on these, living them on a daily basis?	
4. Can (and will) they take us to the next planet? Will they help take your business to a new "planet", achieving your future goals and objectives?	
5. Are they important to the delivery of a positive and consistent experience for our customers? Will they drive the right employee behaviors and actions throughout the customer experience?	
6. Are they important to ensure a positive and engaging experience for my employees? Will they drive the right employee behaviors and actions throughout the employee experience?	

To illustrate this point, here are examples of behaviors from companies I interviewed for this book. They're all behaviors for values that have their roots in the concept of *innovation*, but they define their behaviors in their own meaningful and specific way.

Company	Value	Behaviors
Atlassian	Be the change you seek	All Atlassians should have the courage and resourcefulness to spark change – to make better our products, our people, our place. Continuous improvement is a shared responsibility. Action is an independent one.
giffgaff	Be curious	We talk. We listen. We challenge. We find a better way.
Impraise	Creativity	We embrace unconventional thinking & welcome innovative solutions. ● Find the best way forward ● Seek out different perspectives ● Build on each other's ideas ● Take on challenge & evolve our thinking ● Make time & space to innovate
NAHL Group plc	We are curious	We challenge the status quo, seek to understand our customers and resolve how we could do things better for them.
Propellernet	Innovation	We value innovation as a way of embracing an ever-changing world around us and use it to our advantage, allowing us to reinvent what we do as a business and keep working towards a better tomorrow.
Zappos	Be adventurous, creative and open-minded	Takes risks in alignment with Zappos purpose Thinks EVEN BIGGER Willing to fail (and learn from failure) Acts as an entrepreneur

Design behaviors to address differences

Just as no one value will fuel your company and your people, no one behavior for each value will help employees understand what the value means and how to behave in respect to it. One reason for this is that we all define and interpret words in our own unique way, and the other reason is that within our organizations we have so many differences in our people and in the jobs that they do. And for this reason, it's important to address (and respect) these differences, weaving them into how you define your behaviors.

An example that brings this to life is from when I worked at Reward Gateway, and involves the value *push the boundaries* and the behaviors which define it as follows:

> RG People want tomorrow to be better than today. They want to build a better future through everything they do. They question everything, challenge norms, raise bars and restlessly innovate. They see opportunities years ahead of others. They understand that survival means that the only constant is change. RG People set the agenda. They lead our industry.

As you can see, there is a lot of variety in the behaviors listed for this value, ranging from questioning and challenging norms to being trend-setters by leading the industry. By defining it this way, there is something for everyone, regardless of their job level or function – from me, as HR Leader, designing the most innovative HR programs to engage my workforce, to Will, our fabulous Office Manager, designing welcome messages to put a smile on the faces of anyone who visited the office.

Explain them well

Part of defining your behaviors to address the diversity of your business and workforce involves carefully selecting the words you use, explaining them well. For yourself, will the words you've selected capture the attention and get your important points across? If not, then go back and re-write them, for as Gregg Lederman says in his book *Engaged*, "Normally, the fine print is never read or ignored, but here, the fine print is critical. Documented behaviors that all employees know and do are the pot of gold at the end of the rainbow." And for this reason, you need to put as much effort into selecting the behaviors as explaining them. For if you want your behaviors to help move your employees and your business in the right direction, they need to be as robust and powerful as your values.

> *"Inculcating a core set of behaviors in people, then giving them the latitude to practice those behaviors – well, actually, demanding that they practice them – makes teams astonishingly energized and proactive. Such teams are the best drivers to get you where you need to go."*
>
> — Patty McCord, Author and Former Chief Talent Officer at Netflix, *Powerful*.

Show both sides of behaviors

One last method I wanted to mention that some companies use as a way to ensure their behaviors, and thus values, are truly understood and lived, is by showing employees both sides of the behaviors. They explain what it looks like to live them, and then on the flip side, show the behaviors that the business does not want to see in action.

One example of a company who does this is Missguided, who not only share positive behaviors for each value, but negative behaviors, or what they call "callouts". They do this as they feel it's important to be upfront and call out what is and is not expected of employees.

"This adds a bit of structure and teeth to our behaviors, helping conversations and encouraging the right experience," says Glenn Grayson, Internal Communications & Engagement Partner.

An example can be seen below for their value of *dream big,* where they break out positive and negative behaviors as follows:

Positive behaviors:	Negative behaviors:
• We seek opportunities, push boundaries and think outside the box	• We're not dismissive
	• We're not small-minded
• We innovate using technology, creativity and new ways of working	• We're not disinterested
	• We're not stubborn
• We use evidence and data to make sound commercial decisions	
• We don't fear failure, we use it to learn and grow	

Another example is from C Space, who do this in a slightly different way by breaking out their behaviors for 'when it works' and for 'when it doesn't work'. An example can be seen below for their value of *do what scares you* as follows:

When It Works	When It Doesn't Work
Trying new things, even though they might lead to failure.	**Living** outside of your comfort zone, all the time.
Supporting others to get out of their comfort zones.	**Forging** on alone when you need support.
Embracing opportunities for personal growth.	**Assuming** that if you don't find something scary, nobody else will.

When it comes to this point, it's up to you to decide whether you want to put in writing the flipside behaviors. But whether you decide to do it or not, the flipside behaviors should be addressed head-on in conversations and briefings to ensure that there is complete clarity, and no questions as to which behaviors as C Space say, work and don't work.

The outcome of this step is to be ready to move on to Step 7 (and beyond), feeling comfortable that you have the "right" values and behaviors to help you achieve your purpose, your mission or your vision.

Step 7: Set them free

There's a quote that says, "If you love someone, set them free. If they come back, they're yours; if they don't, they never were." I choose this quote because I believe that's exactly the goal of *setting your values free*, having them embraced and believed in so much that they come back to you time and time again in the actions and decisions made by your employees.

How should I brand my values?

Another way to ensure that your values are noticed and remembered is through the use of branding. Branding is a marketing practice where you create a name, symbol or design that is linked to a product, or in this case, to your values. Over the years, I've found it to be a useful and highly effective technique as it creates a memorable impression, giving your values an identity that your employees will recognize and engage with time and time again.

When interviewing companies for this book, I came across some fantastic examples of branding. And for this reason, for each play in Chapter 6, I've included the image they use for their values, sharing the creative ways that they've brought their values to life through branding. You'll notice from these that some have used colors, others icons, and others, such as KP Snacks, have brought their products into the branding to show the alignment with their business. However they've chosen to do it, I'm sure you'll agree that their branding has certainly created an impact and has helped bring their values to life.

At Lexington Catering, a UK award-winning contract caterer, they've branded their mission and values in a unique and creative way, doing so by using the concept of a family tree. They've done this because they position their employer brand as a growing family and also to link it to the concept of nature, as they're all about natural food and helping the planet.

At CSpace, a Customer Agency, they developed their branding around triangles, using individual triangles to build the icons for each of their precious nine values. Each icon is intended to remind employees of the value, even without words. "We wanted (and felt they deserved) to have a visual language that could be utilized to socialize and celebrate them. Perhaps more of a cross between ancient iconography – and a gem from a Tiffany's jewel case, while still carrying through C Space's typography style and color palette. We still wanted them to feel like 'us'," said Josh Roy, Creative Director.

They focused on graphically depicting the nine values as a collection of individual parts that could also come together as a unit to symbolize the success of a greater whole to reflect them as a business, and the interplay of the values with each other. "The triangular shapes serve us well, and we love how the symbology of how our nine values locked up together share the same shape as a single value. The different gradients of cyan assigned to each create contrast, while still uniting them back to our brand's primary color," said Roy.

The branding of the values has created a shared visual language that attaches all of them to each other – from promotional posters that inspire, to booklets that educate, walls that celebrate – and beyond. By doing this, CSpace believes it will help give their values a springboard for keeping them alive as a business.

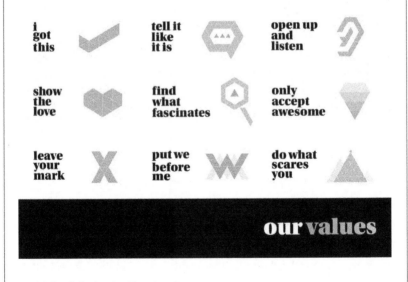

Read the full play in Chapter 6.

The first step in doing this is the launch, or re-launch, of your values, which is an absolutely critical, but often overlooked, part of the process. The other steps, which we'll cover later in the book, are playing with your values (Chapter 3) and keeping your values alive (Chapter 4). Keep in mind that they are all equally important, so don't fool yourself by thinking that once you launch your values you are home free. Similar to the expression "dogs are for life, not just for Christmas", "values are for life, not just for the launch".

Back to the first step, launching/re-launching your values. There is no right or wrong way to do this, for just as values differ from company to company, so too are how you launch them due to differences in the company, culture and the values themselves.

Regardless of what you decide to do, here are a few important areas to cover in your launch/re-launch sessions:

● **Start by explaining your journey; the "why"**

It's important to resist the temptation of starting these sessions out by sharing your new values. For although you may be well aware of why they've been put in place, what you've done to discover them, and why you've selected these values, the majority of your workforce will not. So, take them on the journey, starting with the "why" before moving onto the "what" (what your values area) and the "how" (how they'll be used).

> *"People don't buy what you do; they buy why you do it. And what you do simply proves what you believe."*
>
> – Simon Sinek, *Start with Why: How Great Leaders Inspire Everyone to Take Action*

● **Share stories (lots of them)**

One of the best ways you can, and should, get your important messages across is through stories and storytelling, sharing examples of the values in action. These bring the information to life in a powerful and effective way, and also give it a much better chance of being remembered, and thus actioned.

Research shows that people are more likely to remember a story than a statistic. In a research study conducted at Stanford University, students were asked to give one-minute speeches that contained three statistics and one story. Only 5 percent of the listeners remembered a single statistic, while 63 percent remembered the stories.

Keep in mind that the person telling the stories is just as important as the stories themselves, so think carefully about who will be your storytellers. Consider who will get the most buy-in from your employees – is it a senior leader, a colleague, both? Having them share a story of how they've lived a value or witnessed it being lived, can be so powerful, and can make a monumental difference in you achieving your objectives.

When Charles Tyrwhitt, a men's clothing retailer, launched their new values, their senior leadership team had an active and important role to play throughout the session. They did this by first taking attendees through the journey of how the values were designed, sharing stories and examples of what the values mean to them personally. They next spoke about their personal commitments to each of the beliefs and behaviors, making them more real and relatable to their workforce. And finally, they led group activities before finishing the day by responding to and addressing any concerns that were raised.

Read the full play in Chapter 6

● Get your employees involved

Nothing is worse than sitting through a dull and boring PowerPoint presentation, so why not get your employees involved in living your values from the start, in these sessions? I've seen this done in many fun and outrageous ways, with activities designed to bring your values to life in a much more effective way. So, put on your creative hats, and come up with activities and exercises to get your employees involved.

When MOSL launched their values, they did so by running a "Values Day". During this day out, they had groups discuss what the values mean to them personally, to the team, and to the organization. They then moved onto a stop/start/continue exercise, where they discussed what needed to happen so that the values could be lived each and every day. And finally, the day ended with what they called their 'Challenge 100 competition', which involved fun (and silly) activities which indirectly aligned with the values. The challenges included creative tasks, team tasks, solution-seeking tasks and manual building tasks. Teams were awarded 'fun money', based on how successfully they completed each task, and at the end, the team with the most money won the competition.

Read full play in Chapter 6

And, to help you out a bit more, here are four tips I've learned through the years when it comes to these sessions:

1. **Stay focused on your objectives**

   Keep in mind why you're holding these sessions to begin with, which is to raise awareness of your values, help employees understand them, and create a call to action. Design everything you do for the sessions around these key objectives, so that when you're finished, you've achieved them.

2. **Think of it as a marketing pitch**

   Think of these sessions as a marketing pitch, where you're "selling" your values to your employees. And like any marketing pitch, you want to use any and all marketing tools and approaches you can. In fact, why not invite someone from the Marketing team to come and join your project team so they can work their marketing magic on your behalf?

3. **Don't leave it to the last minute**

   Start thinking, planning and designing your sessions at the start of the process, not leaving it to the last minute. By doing this, you'll end up with something as impactful as the values themselves, and not something that comes across to your employees as rushed or lackluster.

4. **Re-use, recycle, repeat**

You will have put tons of work into these sessions, so don't do it once and then put it away in a drawer. As you're developing them, think of how you can use them in the future for new employees, or as a way to bring back awareness of your values at another time.

TIPS TO PLAY WITH

✪ **Remember that your values are already within you**

Keep in mind that your values are already within you, floating on the surface of how your company and your employees behave, day in and day out. And for this reason, the journey to discover them involves looking at what you already **say**, what you already **do**, what you already **believe**, and what you want and need to **protect**.

✪ **Take your time to get it *right***

There's an expression that "Rome wasn't built in a day", which is fitting when we talk about values, for when it comes to something as important, meaningful and strategic as values, we absolutely need to take our time to build it and get it "right". This could take weeks, months, or even a year, so don't focus on the time, but on the outcome. If you do this, you'll end up with something your company and your workforce are proud of, can live with, and drives the results which are critical to your success.

✪ **Bring others along**

Helen Keller was quoted as saying "Alone we can do so little, together we can do so much." This is true in life, and certainly true when it comes to discovering your values. The more diverse people and thoughts you involve in the process, the better chance you have of discovering the "right" values, getting buy-in and ultimately achieving your business objectives.

✪ Do it with *wow*

The word "wow" means[2] to inspire and excite, to express astonishment or admiration, and to create a sensational success – all great outcomes, and all things we don't just want but need from our values. Find your own way to create wow through your values, doing it in your own way by asking yourself the four questions listed earlier in the chapter: 1) Are they servants to my purpose or mission? 2) Are they specific to my company? 3) Can (and will) they be lived? 4) Can (and will) they take us to the next planet?

---

2   Taken from the Oxford Dictionary.

Playing with your values

Introduction

I love designing gardens, researching which plants to buy, where they should be placed, and how they'll all work together to create a flourishing tapestry to be seen and appreciated throughout the year. But for me, that's where it ends, for as much as I love designing gardens, I despise tending them. This means that unless I hire a gardener, my lovely garden ends up with weeds popping up everywhere, some plants getting too big and overshadowing others; it's an absolute disaster!

The same thing can and will happen if you stop once you discover and design your values and behaviors. For although they may be **the** best values, like a garden, if they aren't nourished, tended and maintained by fully embedding them into each and every thing you do, they'll never flourish. As Rudyard Kipling said, "Gardens are not made by singing 'Oh how beautiful', and sitting in the shade."

Brené Brown, researcher and author, writes in her book *Dare to Lead*, "only about 10 percent of organizations have operationalized their values into teachable and observable behaviors that are used to train their employees and hold people accountable." **No wonder only 23% of employees can apply their values – we aren't making it easy for them!**

> "It's not the content of the ideology that makes a company visionary, it's the authenticity, discipline, and consistency with which the ideology is lived – the degree of alignment – that differentiates visionary companies from the rest of the pack. It's not what you believe that sets you apart, as much as that you believe in something, that you believe in it deeply, that you preserve it over time, and that you bring it to life with consistent alignment."
>
> – Jim Collins and Jerry Porras, *Built to Last*

In this chapter, we'll explore why and how you can *bring your values out to play* at four key touchpoints in the employee experience – hiring, onboarding, recognition and performance management. But before we jump into this, let's first talk about the 'why' for two important concepts – the power of play and the power of habits and cues. This will have an important role in helping to bring your values out to play, and ultimately, helping your values flourish.

The power of play

In *Dare to Lead* by Brené Brown, she talks about *living into* your values, making the point that companies need their employees to not only just live their values, but to take it that one step further by moving the values into actions. This is so important in a world where we all have choices – choices in where to work, how we want to work, and what we want to believe. And it's only when you *live into* something that you choose to invest your valuable time and energy into something as important as your company values.

Wonderful; that's exactly what we need from our employees. But how does this happen? How do we get them to live into and action the company's values? One way is through the concept of play, something that's been proven to be an effective business tool because it improves productivity, innovation and teamwork, all things our companies require to be successful.

But let me point out the obvious, and that is that play will only happen if you have the equipment out for employees to play with. Think of it this way; if your employees are playing a game of basketball, how can they play if you don't have the balls on the court? It's this concept of bringing the equipment out onto the court that is so critical and, unfortunately, is so often overlooked. And it's this concept of bringing your values out to play that we'll be covering throughout this book, helping you discover more ways to use this powerful tool within your company.

The power of habits

One day, I was riding my bike and was hit by a car. It could have ended badly, but because I had been a gymnast since the age of seven, old habits took over, and it actually ended in quite a funny way . . . well at least to me, but probably not so to the driver of the car or onlookers.

Let me explain. After I was hit by the car, I found myself flying through the air, heading towards a very hard and painful landing on the ground. But all of a sudden, my body naturally got into a tuck position and I did a front flip, landing safely on my feet. But it didn't end there, as I didn't just land my flip, but did an Olympic-style perfect 10 landing, surprising the driver of the car and the onlookers who applauded my athletic abilities . . . ok, they didn't really applaud, but in my mind they did!

The reason I'm sharing this story is to illustrate the next power, which is the power of habits, and the difference they can make when they become second nature in how you think and how you act. The stronger the habit, the more automatic it becomes.

Here are some interesting statistics about habits which show two things – they really do make a difference and, unfortunately, habits don't happen overnight.

- 40 percent of your actions are not conscious decisions but habits.
- It can take anywhere from 15 days to 254 days to truly form a new habit.

This is exactly what we want (and need) from our values, which is to have them be automatic reactions, behaviors and actions to our employees. You've designed them to drive your business, so using them to drive actions is paramount to helping your company thrive and survive, in good times and bad!

And the best way to ensure your values become and stay as habits is to bring them out to play, embedding them, or as Elaine Page, Co-Founder and Managing Principal at The Good Trouble Company, says, *plumbing* them into everything you do. By doing this, you'll ensure that if and when your employees 'fall off their bikes', they'll know instinctively what to do and how to act, and achieve that perfect '10' score!

> *"People have well-honed bullshit detectors these days. If the only time people encounter your company's values is on a PowerPoint slide at their induction, they're never going to stick. Values must be lived to be believed, and if they aren't, they'll simply fade away."*
>
> **– Nikki Gatenby,** *Superengaged*

Hiring

You are what you eat

When I was young, my mother used to say to me, "you are what you eat". Strange expression I know, but it basically means that if you want to be fit and healthy you need to eat well. Well, the same is true with our companies; if we want them to be fit and healthy, it all starts with what you put into them, the employees we "feed" into our companies. If we "feed" them the right kind of employees they, in turn, will be right for our companies.

Why am I saying this? Certainly, we all know that it's critical to hire the right people. That's why so many companies are investing heavily in new technology and processes to test and scrutinize candidates based on their technical skills, aptitude, personality and judgement. But is this enough? Doesn't this miss out on **the** most critical part of a 'healthy diet', your company values?

If you truly want a healthy company, it all needs to start and stop with hiring based on your values – getting the right people in the door to begin with.

Making values a non-negotiable

Stephanie was frustrated; she had looked and looked for the perfect candidate and was getting nowhere. And to make matters worse, she was getting pressure from her boss as she was behind in her deliverables, and from her team as they were burdened with extra work.

So, she did what I've heard managers do time and time again, she relaxed her standards when it came to values. She focused on someone who could come in and technically deliver, believing that this was the right decision for her team and for the company.

Wrong, for although they came in and started delivering, they did so at the expense of others on the team. They became a toxic member of the team, one that eventually impacted the quality of the work, and in the end, even forced others to leave the company.

Does this sound familiar? Have you ever been in this situation or witnessed it at your company? If you have, you've probably felt the pain that Stephanie and her team did, with the long-term pain outweighing the short-term gains. For this reason, I'm pleased to say that I'm seeing more companies making values a non-negotiable when it comes to hiring decisions, saying no to anyone who doesn't meet their values criteria.

One example is Nav, a U.S. FinTech company, who have a policy that says that if there are any values-based 'red flags', the candidate cannot be hired, no matter what. They put this policy in place after discovering that every single person leaving before they completed their six-month probation period had been given a values-based red flag in the interview process, meaning the interviewer had noted concerns based on a values fit. This showed them that by overlooking these red flags, they were bringing in people who weren't right for their company and wouldn't last in the long-term.

Read full play in Chapter 6

Resist the urge and make values a non-negotiable in your hiring decisions – say no to anyone and everyone who is not a values fit.

You can't get blood from a stone

And the reason it's important to get the values fit right during the hiring process is, as the expression goes, "you can't get blood from a stone." What I mean by this is that as much as you'd like to, it is extremely difficult to get someone to do something or believe in something which is not in line with who they are and their fundamental beliefs.

> *"Core values (and purpose) are not something people 'buy in' to. People must already have a predisposition to holding them. The task is to find people who already have a predisposition to share them with you."*
>
> **Jim Collins and Jerry Porras,** *Built to Last*

To illustrate this point, let me share with you a personal story. Many years ago, long before I realized the importance of values, I joined a company based on a technical fit – I had the right technical skills for them and they had the right technical work for me. However, we both soon realized that the values fit was absolutely positively wrong, and because of this, I was not the right person for the job or the company!

My boss said to me as I was leaving, "you see too much color for a company that paints using only black and white". It was an important lesson for me as a candidate and as a Human Resource Leader, to always weave values-related questions and discussions into the interview process . . . using color of course!

Getting your questions right

Now that I've made the point about the importance of having a values-led approach to hiring, let's move on to the how. So, how can you get started or improve on how you do this already? Let's start with the questions themselves, looking at how to get them 'right'. Here are a few things to keep in mind:

☐ **Design questions that are specific to each and every one of your values.**

When designing the questions you'll be asking candidates, make sure to address each and every one of your lovely values. Don't leave any of them out, or you'll be missing out on this important and critical part of the process.

☐ **Design questions that address the overlap of your values.**

Just as important as asking questions about each individual value, is asking questions about your values in a more holistic manner. As mentioned earlier in the book, you'll have values that overlap and work together, and this alignment, or at times conflict, is just as critical to explore. For this reason, it's important to design questions where candidates will have to share how they have handled or will handle these situations.

Let's say, for example, you have one value which focuses on safety and another on customer service. Design a question which asks candidates how they would handle a situation when these values conflict; so, for example, a customer wants something that could put them at risk.

☐ **Share values (and questions) in advance.**

Interviews and interview questions are not a way to trip up candidates, but a way for them to present their best selves. For this reason, I'm a firm believer in making sure that candidates have all the facts before they show up, so not just where and when the interview will take place, but how and what will be discussed. As Nikki Gatenby writes in *Superengaged*, "We genuinely want to hear interview candidates' take on our values, so we make sure they've had some time to think about their answers."

A common and effective approach for developing questions that deliver the information and responses you need from candidates is the STAR approach. Here's how it works:

S	T	A	R
Situation	**Task**	**Action**	**Result**
Sets the scene, giving the background or context to the situation.	Describes the purpose, so what was the desired outcome, and what was initially tasked.	Explains what was specifically done to achieve the task.	Shares the outcome as well as how it relates back to the initial task.

The key to this approach, or any other which you may prefer, is to always relate them back to the values, so that you end the interview having a strong understanding of how the candidate interprets each value and also how they have and will display them at your company.

To help you get started, here are some sample interview questions based on two generic values:

Value	Sample questions
Innovation	• What does innovation mean to you?
	• Share an example of how you've recently embraced and put innovation in place.
	• What was the best mistake you've made? Why was it the best mistake? What did you learn from it?
	• If this was your first day on the job and your task was to do xyz, what would you do for those first eight hours to create a more innovative approach/outcome?
Teamwork	• What does teamwork mean to you?
	• Tell me about a time in your recent working life when you had to be diplomatic in your dealings with colleagues, taking them along with you even when you did not agree with their position. What was the situation, where did you disagree, and what was the outcome?
	• How do you earn the trust of colleagues?
	• Tell me about a time when you had to admit your mistakes to your colleagues.

Setting your assessors up for success

The final, and often overlooked step for ensuring that you have an effective values-led hiring process involves training your assessors on how to conduct values-based interviews. Never assume that by giving them a list of interview questions, they will magically know how to ask and assess candidates against them, for trust me, this will not happen!

Instead, set your assessors (and your company) up for success by helping them understand why you're using this approach and why their role is so important. And then, give them the tools and support to make sure they're comfortable and ready to go.

At Atlassian, an enterprise software company, they select and train a group of people who are used specifically as values assessors during the selection process. The rationale behind this is that "interviewing, in general, is a muscle that not everyone has, and values interviews specifically are that much harder," says Dominic Price, Work Futurist.

They select those that are role models in how they live and breathe their values, and then train them on how to ask questions to determine if candidates would be able to live their values and add to their culture.

Read full play in Chapter 6

TIPS TO PLAY WITH

✪ **No excuses, do it!**

If you don't have a values-based approach to hiring currently, don't wait any longer, start doing it now! Even if it's simply adding a few values-based questions to what you normally do, this will at least move you in the right direction to start making decisions based on your values.

✪ **Focus on asking the right questions**

Albert Einstein said that "If I had an hour to solve a problem and my life depended on it, I would use the first 55 minutes determining the proper question to ask, for once I know the proper question, I could solve the problem in less than 5 minutes."

So, if you want to get the right answers to your questions, start by asking the right questions. Focus on ones that will help you see candidates under the 'values spotlight', showcasing who they truly are and the contribution they'll make. Keep in mind that not all jobs require the same level of living the values, so make sure the questions are designed to focus on the right ones in the right amount of detail.

✪ Peel candidates like an onion

Carl Sandburg said that "Life is like an onion. You peel it off one layer at a time, and sometimes you weep."

So, if you don't want to weep because you've hired the wrong candidates, peel away at the different layers of your candidate's values-based responses to make sure you're at the core of who they are and how they will ultimately behave.

✪ Don't sugar-coat your values (or your culture)

And finally, remember that you're not just bringing your values out to play so that you can assess your candidates, you're also doing it so that the candidate can assess you. So, be as open as possible as soon as possible in the recruitment process to showcase and discuss your values. By doing this, you have a much better chance of getting the right fit so that you don't make a critical hiring mistake, wasting your valuable time and money.

See it in action

Read more about how companies are doing values-based hiring in the following plays in Chapter 6:

- Addison Lee Group
- Atlassian
- Blue Lagoon Iceland
- Decathlon
- Deloitte
- Dishoom
- Events DC
- ICC Sydney
- Inspired Villages
- Nav
- Starred
- TrustFord
- WD-40 Company

Put your values in the starting lineup

Onboarding is one of those important signature moments. It's a time when your new employee is reminded of why they decided to join your company, setting the tone, direction, and ultimately your new employee up for success.

And that's why it is absolutely critical to take your values 'off the bench' and put them in the starting lineup throughout your onboarding program. If you only take them out to hand out a pretty document listing your values (which has happened to me), or by spending five minutes reading them out loud from a PowerPoint presentation (which has happened to me), it will absolutely positively do nothing to help you "win the game". Why? Well, continuing with the sports analogy, if your employees aren't clear that your values are a critical part of "playing the game", they too will keep them on the sidelines as they won't see them as worth remembering or using.

Your values deserve to be in the starting lineup of your onboarding program – not sitting on the sidelines waiting to be called into action.

At Reward Gateway, they share their values with employees on day one by giving them each a welcome box. The contents of the box have been thoroughly planned out to align with the company's purpose, mission, and values to show the Reward Gateway culture 'in a box'.

Read the full play in Chapter 6

Help your employees understand the true meaning

Once you've made the decision to take your values "off the bench" and use them as an integral part of your onboarding program, the next important decision is, how will you do this? How will you present your values in such a way that new employees will understand their true meaning, what they mean to them and to the business, and how they should be used day in and day out?

What's important here is teaching and not telling, making sure that new employees walk away from onboarding knowing not just what the words mean, but how they can and should impact their actions and behaviors. So, throw away those boring, and ineffective PowerPoint presentations and consider some or all of the following as ways to help your employees learn to truly understand and live your values:

- **Get your senior leaders involved.**

  A great way to signal to new employees that your values are important and should be taken seriously is by bringing senior leaders into the onboarding process. Have them talk about what the values mean to them personally and to the business. Have them share a story about a time when a value has helped them, or a time when they put a value before profit, thus showing that the company means business in their values. And finally, have them share a story of when they felt they had gone wrong by ignoring or missing a value, as stories of personal struggle and failure are often more powerful than those involving success.

- **Have employees share stories.**

  It's not just leaders who can and should share stories about what the values mean to them and how they've brought them to life, as hearing stories from fellow colleagues can be just as powerful. So, invite some along to your onboarding sessions, and help new employees learn firsthand what it looks like to live the values.

- **Have new employees share stories.**

  You've hired these new employees because you believe they're right for the job, and have demonstrated in the interview that they're a values fit. So why not have them share with each other what they've done already to live the values, as well as how they think they'll do so at your company? It's a great way to get them talking, and *fishing*, with your values from day one.

- **Play some games.**

  Another great way to get employees *fishing* with your values is to have a bit of fun with them by playing games. You may have done this when you launched your values, so borrow from these, or if you didn't, create some new ones that align with your values. For example, if you have a value about innovation, play a game using the behaviors required for innovation. I love the game when you give each team a bag of marshmallows and a bag of pasta and see who can build the highest structure, but there are tons of others that do the same thing and get people playing and not just talking about your values.

If you want your employees to truly live (and play) with your values, it needs to start with them learning both what they mean and how to use them, giving them life and personality from day one.

Overcoming old memories and behaviors

So far, I've spoken about the importance of teaching your values throughout the onboarding process as a way to introduce and embed your values from day one. But there's one more important reason for bringing your values out to play during onboarding, and that's because it helps overcome what cognitive psychologists call "proactive interference". This is what happens when you can't learn a new task because your old memories, behaviors and ways of working prevent you from doing so.

For example, let's say you just joined a company which has a value which talks about being innovative and creative. At your last company, you didn't have this value, so it's not something that you are comfortable with or may even know how to do. What this means is that to be successful at your new company, you will need to overcome your old habits and behaviors, and learn new ones based on expectations of behaving in an innovative and creative way.

The good news is that you can overcome these old memories and behaviors. The bad news is that if doesn't happen early on, during onboarding, you risk employees being stuck in the past, living values that may indeed conflict with your company values. So, get in there early, and help and support your new employees on their learning (and behaving) journey.

Comma Group, an international management consultancy focused exclusively on data and information management, have created a values exercise as part of their graduate training program. Instead of going through the values in a classroom setting, graduates are tasked with going around the business to find out from colleagues what the values are and what they mean. This process helps graduates learn and understand the values in an interactive and effective way.

"In setting this exercise, we hope that our values will endure in the minds of the next generation of Comma Consultants, and that they will gain a deeper understanding of the behaviors that so much of our success is reliant upon. We were pleasantly surprised (relieved) that the value statements produced by the graduates bore many similarities to our actual company value statements. Not only does this exercise provide a valuable learning experience for our trainees, but it also helps us gauge whether we as a company are behaving in accordance with the values that we would like to be known for – a true test of our success!" says Mike Evans, Chief Technology Officer.

TIPS TO PLAY WITH

✪ **No excuses, do it!**

If your values are not a part of your onboarding program currently, don't wait any longer, start doing it now! There are lots of simple and effective ways to do this, so check out the plays mentioned below to get inspiration.

✪ **Make it intentional**

If your values do not have a starting spot on the onboarding line-up, they are not intentional, they are merely sitting on the bench waiting to be called on to play. They need to be prominent throughout your onboarding process so that employees can see and hear from day one that they are important to the company and to them.

✪ **Share stories**

As you can tell from this book, and my previous books, I am a bit of a storyteller. And that's because I believe that we learn more from stories than from anything else. So, tell as many stories as you can to bring your values to life, and while you're at it, go out there and find employees to join your onboarding sessions and share their stories of what the values mean to them and how they live them. Trust me, they'll love sharing their stories as much as your new employees will love hearing them!

See it in action

Read more about how these companies are doing this in Chapter 6:

- Addison Lee Group
- Blue Lagoon Iceland
- Events DC
- ICC Sydney
- Inspired Villages
- Reward Gateway
- TrustFord
- Valor Hospitality
- Zappos

Recognition

Superheroes versus Supervillains

Whenever I speak on the topic of recognition, I always start out by talking about the power of recognition, how it can lead to positive results for your company and, as Gregg Lederman says in his book *Crave*, how it can give employees what they crave.

> Companies who have effective recognition programs have **14% better** employee engagement, productivity and customer service than those without – *Bersin* by Deloitte

Through the power of recognition, 'normal' employees can be turned into what I call **superheroes**. Now they may not be able to leap tall buildings or lift a bus, but they can and will be able to perform and achieve spectacular results for your business.

Let me pause for a moment and throw in a 'but' (my husband's second least favorite word right after 'just'), and that is to point out that if recognition is not done in the 'right' way, then you risk creating supervillains instead of superheroes. **And the key to doing recognition 'right' is linking it to your values.**

To understand this better, think of any action film you've ever seen when a superhero has gone bad. Suddenly, they lose their focus and desire to use their powers for good and begin using their powers in destructive ways. The same will happen at your company if you don't recognize, and thus reinforce, the superpowers that you want your employees to exhibit, showing them time and time again what good looks like.

And if you think that these supervillains only come out in films, all you have to do is look at what happened at companies such as Enron, an example used over and over again, where supervillains (evil employees) take over the company and completely destroy it. What would have happened if they had embraced their values, being recognized for them, seeing that this was what was expected and rewarded? I believe that the end of the 'film' would have been very different!

Here are some statistics that show the power of values-based recognition:

- Companies with values-based recognition are **two times** more likely to reinforce and drive business results – SHRM
- Employees at companies with values-based recognition are **four times** more likely to say they believe in their values – SHRM

Getting recognition 'right'

Recognizing against values can and will vary greatly from company to company based on what your values are, and your culture in general. However, in reviewing the companies that get recognition 'right', here are a few common themes to keep in mind:

- **Make it a part of the culture**

  One of the biggest barriers I've seen at companies when it comes to recognition is that they don't have a recognition culture, where giving praise is something that is considered natural and a part of how they work. You need to overcome this first, helping and working with leaders and employees to understand why and how to recognize.

- **Make it meaningful**

  Another challenge with recognition is that if it isn't done in a meaningful way, it won't come across as genuine and it won't be effective. A simple 'thank you' just doesn't cut it; it needs to do more by answering these three questions, or what I call the three 'what's:

  1. **What value(s)** have they been recognized for?
  2. **What behavior** have they exhibited which is being recognized?
  3. **What difference** did their behavior make to the company?

  If you don't do this, then how in the world will your employees know what they've done to live their values, **and** the difference that it's made to the company? They deserve to know so that they know (and can repeat) what good is, and your business deserves to know so that they get these positive results time and time again.

● Make it continuous

If you want your employees to truly understand your values and then, more importantly, action them, you need to start by recognizing against them on a continuous basis. Recognizing every quarter or every year, which is a common practice, is good, but is it good enough? If employees only hear these messages every quarter or every year, will the message get across? Absolutely not, so weave it into your recognition program on a continuous and ongoing basis.

● Put it under the spotlight

As human beings, we are wired to be competitive, meaning if we see someone else get something, basically we want it. Case in point, have you ever ordered something on a restaurant menu and then when your friend's order arrives, you're jealous that you didn't order it yourself?

So why not leverage this as a way to create more superheroes to fight your enemies through putting values-based recognition under the spotlight? If your employees see others being recognized for living a value, they'll not only understand the values better, but understand (and strive for) the behaviors that will get them noticed, appreciated, recognized.

Recognizing in your own way

Just as you design values that are unique to you and your organization, the same is true when it comes to recognition. I've worked at many companies throughout my career, and not once did we recognize in the same way, although they were all based on values.

In Chapter 6, you'll find many examples of how companies do this. But just to make sure you have enough inspiration, I've shared below four more examples that don't appear in the plays. I'm sure you'll agree that they've all recognized their employees against their values in their own unique and amazing way.

Nav

At Nav, they give out t-shirts for living their values. They went with t-shirts for as Levi King, CEO & Co-Founder explained, "We're not a workplace of plaques and certificates, we are t-shirt kind of people." Their laid-back dress code means most people are wearing Nav t-shirts regularly anyway, so giving out another

t-shirt just felt like something people would not only wear, but want. And, as King says, "Having the t-shirts worn by folks is an ongoing reminder to not only themselves but others about the values we want to uphold and the people that emulate them."

Tony's Chocolonely

They have a 'Because we can-can' award which recognizes living their core value of being entrepreneurial. The winner receives an engraved glass watering can to use that quarter.

Radio Flyer

They give out golden wagons, which are miniature replicas of one of their products, as a way to recognize one another for living the company values. The wagons are passed from one employee, or what they call "Flyers",

to another each month along with a handwritten "you are awesome" note. The recipient of the wagon adds their initials on the bottom of the wagon before passing it on, as yet another way to track and celebrate their achievements.

TIPS TO PLAY WITH

✪ **No excuses, do it!**

If you don't have a values-based recognition program currently, don't wait any longer, just do it! There are lots of simple and effective ways to do this, so check out the plays mentioned below to get inspiration.

✪ **Make it specific, continuous, and put it under the spotlight**

If you want to get recognition right, and who doesn't, then follow the three tips I shared earlier in this section. Go back and check that your program ticks the box against all of them, and if it doesn't, then go back and change it.

✪ **Do it in your own way**

The reason I share so many examples is that I want to showcase how you can (and must) do things in your own unique way. Go back and check that you've added what makes you special into your recognition program, using it to help you stand out and be yourself.

✪ **Have some fun**

The great thing about recognition is that it's an area where you can (and should) have a bit of fun. And if you want inspiration, again, check out the examples I shared previously or in the plays I've referenced below.

See it in action

Read more about how these companies are doing this in Chapter 6:

- Addison Lee Group
- Charles Tyrwhitt
- Credit Union Australia
- Deloitte
- Dishoom
- Impraise
- Inspired Villages
- KidZania London
- KP Snacks
- NAHL Group plc
- Reward Gateway
- St John Ambulance
- Starred

Performance management

Give your values a starring role

Earlier in this chapter, I suggested that you put your values in the *starting lineup* of your onboarding program, meaning that you don't keep them on the bench, only bringing them out from time to time. Let me take it that one step further when it comes to performance management, and say that you not only need to take your values off the bench, but moving from a sport to a theatre analogy, you need to give them a *starring role* in your performance management program.

Too often, companies leave their values out of the performance management process, instead focusing merely on results, so the objectives that are to be achieved. And while it is important to have a focus on the what, it is just as important to focus on the how, which are your values and behaviors. By leaving them out of the performance management process, you are signaling to your employees that the priority is achieving results, no matter how they get there.

Only 2 in 10 employees say their performance is managed in a way that motivates them to do outstanding work. – Gallup study

Not surprising, for if performance is only managed against the what (objectives) and not the how (values and behaviors), I ask, can this really be motivational?

Stimulate the right conversations

Key to giving your values a starring role in the performance management process is, using the theatre analogy again, giving them *lines*. What I mean by this is that it's not enough to put someone on stage, they have to say and do things that are going to make them stand out, make a difference and an impact, and that's exactly what can and will happen if you use your values to drive the right conversations.

And some of the best conversations that will happen if you integrate your values into performance management are those that provide employees with feedback on how they're living the values, or, as the WD-40 Company says on their performance appraisal form, if they're "just visiting them". By providing this important feedback, employees will be clear as to which behaviors align with the values and which require further development to keep them on track. If this doesn't happen, employees will be left to guess whether or not they are meeting the needs and expectations of their manager and the business.

As Patrick Lencioni says in his book, *The Advantage,* "The best performance management programs are designed to stimulate the right conversations around the right topics". And that's exactly what happens when you give your values a starring role in your performance management process, as it brings conversations centered and focused around your values and behaviors to the stage over and over again.

What gets measured gets done

There's a saying that "what gets measured gets done", meaning that if you give something focus and attention by measuring it, you have a better chance of it being done. And when it comes to your values, that's exactly what you need, that focus and attention to say that they matter. That it's not just about the results, but how you get to the results.

But how do you know how much emphasis you should put on values? How much weight should you give them compared to other performance management measurements or elements? The answer to these questions is that it depends. It depends on how well your values are embedded in your processes and your ways of working, how well they are led by your leaders and lived by your workforce, and even how your values fit into everything else you believe in and do at your company.

To illustrate this, here are four examples of how companies are using values as an integral part of their performance management process in different ways. If you want to read more about how they do this, you can go to their individual plays which can be found in Chapter 6.

1. Atlassian	**2. Charles Tyrwhitt**
They have three equally weighted elements:	They have two equally weighted elements:
1) Expectations of the role – 33.3% 2) Contribution to the team – 33.3% 3) *Demonstration of the values – 33.3%*	1) How they deliver against their objectives – 50% 2) *How they behave against their values – 50%*

3. KP Snacks	4. WD-40 Company
They have two elements which are weighted as follows:	They have three equally weighted elements:
1) Achieving objectives – 70% 2) Demonstrate the values – 30%	1) How well they achieve their essential functions – 33.3% 2) How well they achieve their goals and initiatives – 33.3% 3) How well they live their values – 33.3%

Make it clear and easy

It's all well and good to assess against values and behaviors, but if it's not done in the right way, all it will do is confuse, frustrate and disengage employees. So, if you're going to include values in your performance management process (which I hope you do), then make sure to take the time to develop clear descriptions, criteria and guidance that can be used to drive the right conversations and drive a fair and consistent process.

Saying goodbye

I couldn't end this section on performance management without address-ing the *elephant in the room*, which is the topic of what to do if/when an employee isn't living your values. It's something I've seen happen way too often, and when it does, it erases all the great work that's been done to create a values-led business and at the same time, sends a message that you aren't serious about your values.

Sadly, where this happens the most is when it comes to high performers, or as Reed Hastings and Patty McCord call them 'brilliant jerks' in the infamous Netflix Culture Deck. You know them, your best salesperson or your most talented developer, those people that you just can't bear to lose or they'll bring down the entire company. But at what cost? Are you willing to negatively influence the performance of those around them, those who have embraced and are living your values? And are you willing to have them walk out the door?

As Hastings says in the Netflix Culture Deck, "Brilliant jerks. Some companies tolerate them. For us, cost to effective teamwork is too high." So be brave, and fire those brilliant jerks before it's too late.

TIPS TO PLAY WITH

✪ **Give your values a starring role in performance management**

If you want your employees to truly live (and play) with your values, you need to give them a starring role in your performance management process, signaling to employees that they are a main character in how they are being asked to perform and behave. This also puts them in the center of conversations, making them an integral and ongoing part of the language being used and the behaviors being followed.

✪ **Train and support it**

If you're going to give your values this starring role, make sure your entire workforce is equipped with the training and tools required to perform well. Train it, provide support documents, whatever it takes to set them up to successfully use their values.

✪ **Put your money where your mouth is**

And finally, once you give your values a starring role, "pay" them for this. For although it's fine to at first weave them into the performance management conversations, your goal should be to weave them into the decisions surrounding performance ratings and pay increases. This is key in moving them from having a supporting to a starring role.

See it in action

Read more about how these companies are doing this in Chapter 6:

- Atlassian
- Charles Tyrwhitt
- Deloitte

- Credit Union Australia
- WD-40 Company
- Zappos

CHAPTER 4

Keeping your values alive

CHAPTER OBJECTIVES

In this chapter, we'll cover:

- Why it's important to keep your values alive.
- How you can keep your values alive in different ways.

Introduction

In the last chapter, I started with the analogy of a garden, saying that like a garden, values need to be nourished, tended and maintained by fully embedding them into each and every thing you do so that they flourish. But what happens when you forget or find yourself too busy to water your garden? Yes, you may have a very well-tended garden, no weeds in sight, but unfortunately, your plants will have withered and died off as they haven't had the water to keep them alive.

The same is true with your values, for if you don't constantly and continually use them, they too will wither away, disappearing into your history books. And while embedding and using them in the touchpoints explained in the last chapter is a great start, it is not the end. You need to put as much, if not more, energy into bringing your values out to play time and time again. For if this doesn't happen, the problem I mentioned in the Introduction of only 23 percent of employees strongly agreeing that they can apply their organization's values to their work, will never go away!

> *"The launch is easy – any fool can launch values as it's easy to get attention for something that is new and a bit different. The real work isn't in the launch, it's in the ongoing, never-ending, day in, day out communications and embedding in the fabric of the organization."*
> – Glenn Elliott.

One key reason why you need to constantly and continually bring your values out to play is because of a simple fact – as humans, **we easily forget things**. In fact, according to research on the forgetting curve[3], we forget things quite quickly! Within one hour, your employees will have forgotten on average 50 percent of the information you shared with them. Within 24 hours, they will have forgotten on average 70 percent of the information, and within a week, they will have forgotten on average 90 percent of it. That's a lot of forgetting of information we need our employees to remember and act on!

Another reason is that no matter how good we are at retaining our employees, we all have to face the challenge of turnover and new employees. If we don't keep bringing our values out to play, new employees will have missed all of the great work that you've done in the past.

The good news is that "watering" your garden can actually be a lot of fun, giving you the opportunity to be creative and do things in your own unique way. The key is to find ways to create symbolic reminders of your values, ways to make them visible, reminding your employees over and over again what they are, what they mean, and how and why they should be living them. I call these **VMM**, or **values memory moments**, which act as signals or signposts to your employees.

If you are truly going to commit to a set of values, you need to have a relentless and uncompromising commitment to use them time and time

---

3 The Curve of Forgetting was originally called The Ebbinghaus Curve after the German philosopher, Hermann Ebbinghaus, who developed it in 1885.

again. Fill your "watering can" with VMM (values memory moments) and use them continually to help your plants (company) grow and thrive.

One thing to keep in mind, and my one "but", is to make sure that you are not "pushy" in how you do this. Going back to some of the decision-making tips I gave in Chapter 2 when I spoke about discovering your values, ask yourself if by doing this it will help or hurt your quest to raise awareness of your values. Remember, you only have so many chances before your employees say "enough is enough" and tune out, so use your VMM wisely and strategically.

7 examples of bringing your values out to play

So, let's start playing. In this section, I've shared seven high-level examples of how you can bring your values out to play. Keep in mind that this is not an exhaustive list, but is intended to give you a flavor of what I'm suggesting and, at the same time, inspire you to go out and do it in your own way. And, if you want more examples and more inspiration, and who doesn't, then check out the plays in Chapter 6.

1. Put them where people live

Many companies I've spoken to weave their values into the workplace, whether that's in where they read, drink or sit, as you'll see in the examples below. They do this so that employees are exposed to the values time and time again, in overt and subtle ways, to show employees that the company values are integral to their business, their way of working, and thus to their actions.

Here are four examples from companies included in the plays in Chapter 6:

● **Put your values in your email footer**

At St John Ambulance, they've made their values a part of the email footer. This means that every time an employee receives an email, they have a subtle VMM (visual memory maker) of their values. And since, according to one study[4], on average people receive 120 emails a day, that's a lot of VMMs!

- **Put your values on your employee IDs**

  At KidZania, they put their values on the flip side of the employee ID's which their employees wear around their necks. By doing this it shows employees that their values are there for them, close at hand when they need a reminder.

- **Put your values in your coffee cups**

  At C Space, they put their values logos inside their coffee cups. This way every sip an employee takes reminds them of their values. It's a simple and tasty idea!

- **Put your values on your cushions**

  At Propellernet, they put their values on their cushions. So, not only do your values help you perform better, but they provide comfort at the same time!

- **Put your values in your meeting rooms**

  At the NBA, their meeting rooms are named after each of their values. This is a subtle reminder of them as you walk by or sit in one of these rooms.

2. Create a culture/values book or deck

Started by Zappos, a company famous for their innovative approach to culture and values, culture and values books have become a great tool that companies use for sharing, with potential and existing employees, important details on who they are and what their values are. I've used them many times over my career, and they are a helpful way of putting in

4 Source: Campaign Monitor

employee's hands' reminders of what their values mean and how to put them into action.

Another popular way is through culture decks, with the most well-known one being the 2001 Netflix Culture and Values Deck, which has been downloaded around 19 million times. You can find the Netflix one, along with many other wonderful examples, on this website: https://tettra.co/culture-codes/culture-decks/

3. Put them on your intranet

With more and more companies putting in place company intranets as a way to bring all of their company and people communications together under one platform, this is another great place to showcase your values. Since employees will be on this platform time and time again, having them here will put them under the spotlight.

An example of a company doing this is MOSL. Their values have a prominent spot on their intranet, which they call 'My MO' – meaning my market operator or my modus operandi (MO). On it, they also share a 'Why are values so important' video starring ERIC, which is the acronym used for their four values.

4. Put them on your company website

For this one, I'm not going to name and shame, but let's just say that when I was doing research for this book, I went on quite a few well-known company websites to find their values and …. I couldn't find them anywhere! And if I can't find them, and I'm pretty good at knowing where to look, then how will your potential candidates and clients?

Your values need to be an integral part of your external marketing, including prominently displaying them on your company website. This not only showcases to your potential candidates who you are and why they should join your company, but also it showcases them to your customers, helping them see who you are and how you will impact and drive your service to them. So, if you're not doing this now, quickly stop reading this book and ask your Marketing team to get onto it immediately.

5. Share those lovely stories

Who doesn't love a good story, right? That's the reason that more than half of this book is filled with stories, and why you should do the same when it comes to your values. You hopefully would have already shared stories when you launched your values, but don't stop there; keep those stories coming. They are such a great way to create what are called 'sticky' memories as there's an emotional connection and engagement that makes you want to read and remember them.

And when it comes to values storytelling, this is where you need to leverage your workforce, or as the phrase goes, "let the network do the work". Stories are so much more powerful when they come from colleagues, being heard and actioned in ways that people like me in Human Resources could never dream of achieving. And besides, your employees will have stories that you would have never thought of, signaling that it's OK to live values in different ways.

One way that many of the companies I interviewed do this is by creating values videos starring their employees. In these videos, employees talk about what the values mean to them personally, and how they use them in their jobs. These simple yet effective videos act as a great way to engage your workforce and create a further connection with the values.

And it doesn't have to be just one-off values videos, why not consider doing a values video competition? This is something we introduced when I worked at Merlin Entertainment, where each year, teams created short videos to share their story of what a value(s) meant to them, and then a winner was selected. They were not only fun for the teams to create, fun to watch, but also a great way to get people talking about, and excited about, values.

6. Get creative (and have some fun)

At the start of this chapter, I suggested that you get creative in how you bring your values out to play as it's a great way to drive engagement. Throughout this book, I have and will be sharing examples of how companies do just this to inspire you and your teams, but before I end this chapter, I thought I'd share two more that I'm sure you'll agree are both creative and fun.

● Take your values on a scavenger hunt

At Impraise, they decided to use their values as the basis for a team-building activity, by having a values scavenger hunt. Each team was named after one of their six values, and they did fun, values-related activities. Another company, IIH Nordics, did a similar activity, having their employees throughout the scavenger hunt take photos to creatively illustrate each of their four values.

● Make your employees hungry (and thirsty) for your values

At Missguided, they decided to give their values a starring role at their 10-year company anniversary celebration. So, they did what any "normal" company would do, and created values cocktails and burgers.

"We introduced a culinary-comms™ concept as we wanted to take the idea of embedding our values to the next level. By doing this, we got colleagues to be hungry to live our Vibes (what they call their values) through vibe-themed food and beverages. A tasty way to share messaging and a great treat at the same time." said Glenn Grayson, Internal Communications & Engagement Partner.

VIBE COCKTAILS

LOVE LOTS MARTINI
Passionate martini made with pride

WIN TOGETHER WINTER MOJITO
Berry nice mojito made with zesty win-ter berries

BELIEVE ALWAYS G&T
Classic gin and tonic served with orange peel and rosemary

DREAM BIG G&T
Dreamy pink gin served with raspberries, strawberries and tonic

7. Assess how they're being lived

Keeping your values alive also involves keeping an eye on how your employees are actually living them, understanding where you may have gaps in knowledge or abilities that may need to be addressed. An example of a company which is doing this is Oracle, who have a data-driven approach. Here's what they do:

One of the things that's helped Oracle, global cloud computing provider, excel in the marketplace over the years is their ability to pragmatically reflect on where they are, and where they need to go. This same approach and mindset is used when it comes to how they reflect on their ability to live their values, doing so by assessing the strengths and weaknesses of each of their individual values.

This is done by having each employee complete a self-assessment to identify their strengths and weaknesses for each competency in order to create an employee profile. These profiles are rolled up to paint a picture of the organization's overall strengths and weaknesses which is used to identify and create additional support and development tools for the organization. The profiles are also used as a way for managers to support employees in creating individual development plans to strengthen their weaker competencies. Alignment with the values and direction of the organisation are also surveyed on an annual basis and reported to ensure that communication and training remain focused and appropriate to the needs of the employees.

Oracle's data-driven approach helps create a meaningful and actionable plan for improving the individual and company's ability to fully and effectively live their company values.

Create values champions to promote your values

I couldn't end this chapter without talking about values champions or values committees. I've used these at previous companies, as have many of the companies I interviewed, and they can be the difference between values being truly embraced and those that quietly sit on the sidelines. Here are a few things to keep in mind if you have, or are considering having champions:

● **Think about the selection process**

There is no right or wrong way to select your values champions. Some companies ask for volunteers, others select those that have been recognized for living their values, and some do a combination. Whatever you decide, make sure that you end up with a diverse group to represent your diverse workforce, having people at different job levels, time at the company, and locations. By doing this, you have more "feet on the ground" as the expression goes, so people out there who can truly help to keep your values alive.

● **Be clear about expectations**

Both during the selection process and throughout their time as values champions, it's important to be clear on what you expect of your champions. Spell out their responsibilities, helping to set them up to succeed in this important role.

KP Snacks does this by sharing these four responsibilities of their V&B champions (values & behaviors):

⊃ Endorse and act as a role model for the values & behaviors
⊃ Feedback things that are working well and not working well
⊃ Generate ideas to make values and behaviors real everyday
⊃ Share best practice from other champions and locations

● **Provide training and support**

Equally important in helping your champions succeed, is to provide them with the training and support they need in this role. If you just throw them in, which I have seen done, it's a waste of their time and energy, and you won't accomplish what you need to.

Companies such as KP Snacks hold an annual event where they bring their champions together to provide ongoing training and support, as well as discuss how the values are being lived by their colleagues. This is great for their development, to brainstorm new ideas, and, just as important, to thank and recognize them for their contributions.

TIPS TO PLAY WITH

✪ **Plan it and do it!**

With so many ways to keep your values alive by bringing them out to play, it could get challenging and confusing. So, my first tip is to come together at the start of the year and create a values calendar. With this, you can map out what you'll do and when you'll do each values-related activity, giving you a better chance of ensuring that what you do is strategically designed and intentionally delivered.

✪ **Create VMM in your own way**

As I've said time and time again throughout this book, it's important to do things in your own way, so in this case, to create your own VMMs (values memory moments). Think about the best ways that things get done at your company, follow some, and, mix in some surprises to create the wow you need when it comes to values.

✪ **Have some fun**

Last, but certainly not least, is to go out there and have some fun when you bring your values out to play through your VMM. In this chapter, I've shared ideas, from coffee mugs to cushions to cocktails, to show you that having fun can be just as effective as other more traditional routes. So be creative and find your own ways to have a bit of fun, balancing it with the basics and foundation that you need to create that perfect blend that will bring your values alive and drive home your key messages.

CHAPTER 5

Leading from the top

CHAPTER OBJECTIVES

In this chapter, we'll cover:

- Why your leaders need to lead using your values.
- How you can support your leaders to understand their role and be held accountable.

Introduction

Let me start out by saying that this is one of the shortest chapters in the book. It's not because it's the least important topic, or because there is little to say, but because the points to make are straightforward and to the point. In fact, if I had to sum up this chapter in a few words it would be that it **all starts and stops from the top, with our leaders**.

What I mean by this is that you have absolutely no chance of having your workforce embrace and live your values if your leaders are not passionate, aligned with and living them. No one will ever follow a leader if they do not show through their actions that their promises of living the values are empty.

Now, this may seem obvious; of course we know this, but too often throughout my career, I've seen leaders ignoring the company values and living their own personal set. Here's a real-life example of this:

Sam was an amazing salesperson. He'd shown time and time again that he could win over potential clients, getting them over the finish line, and making the big sale. And for this reason, the company promoted him to be a manager, believing that he would be great at teaching and coaching the more junior members of the team, showing them how he worked his magic, and helping the company succeed.

The only problem was that, although Sam knew what his company values were, he ignored them, doing things in his own way, which were often completely against the values. And since he was successful, and was thus rewarded for these actions, he thought to himself – why bother living the company values?

As an individual contributor, this was bad, but as a manager, a leader, his actions had a wider impact on his team and the company. His team were faced with the challenge of trying to decide who and what to follow – should they stay true to the company values or to Sam's? And if they decided to follow the company values, how would they know how to do this if their manager was not role-modeling them? How would they be recognized and rewarded for living them if their manager didn't even care about them? And finally, how could they stay at a company where the values, something they joined the company because they believed in, were mere words?

This is exactly the scenario created when leaders are not embracing your values, and quite frankly, something that needs to end. So, in this chapter, I'll be sharing how you can help your leaders understand and fulfill the important and critical role they have to play.

Who are our leaders?

85% of people surveyed said that their company relies explicitly on their CEO to reinforce their values. 77% said that such support was one of the 'most effective' practices for reinforcing the company's ability to act on its values. – Booz Allen Hamilton study.

The study cited above shows that employees believe that their CEO has an important role to play in reinforcing their company values. Great, but it has to be so much more than your CEO who is leading the charge if your workforce is going to believe, live and act on your values. They need the support of each and every person who has responsibility for leading and thus influencing others.

When I interviewed Breckon Jones, Head of Performance, Reward, Workforce Analytics & HR Operations at Deloitte, he called these people "megafauna", which is normally a term used when referring to big animals such as elephants. But in this context, it refers to the high-profile people who your workforce looks up to, who will be the charismatic champions and advocates of your values. These are your leaders, and who your workforce will look to for direction when living your values.

> "WD-40 Company embodies the values from the top down because they know values-driven leadership is an inside-out job. Only then can they inspire employees to become caretakers of the brand and protectors of the culture."
>
> **– Garry Ridge, CEO of WD-40 Company.**

Ways to help your leaders

In the same way that we cannot expect our employees to wake up in the morning and magically understand how to live our values, we cannot expect our leaders to wake up and magically understand how to role-model them. This is something we need to help them with, helping them understand the role they play, giving them the support they need, and finally, holding them accountable for doing so.

Have them understand their role

The first thing to do is to make sure that your leaders are clear as to what you expect of them. Something as vague as "we expect you to live the values" just won't work, it will sound like fluffy and meaningless words. If you want them to live your values day in and day out, good days and bad, make it clear how they can, and should, do this and make it clear that they set the tone. For this reason, any time you promote or bring on board a new leader, make this a key part of their development and onboarding.

To help you with this, I have no list to share with you, as the definition of their role will differ based on how you use your values at your company. For example, how do you use them throughout the employee experience, and how do your values translate into business actions? Once you are clear on this, take your leaders through these steps, using all of the tips I've used throughout the book, and their role will become much clearer.

"Leading from the front and living the values creates a guiding cultural light for the whole business to follow, giving the values value, right from the start."

– Nikki Gatenby, Owner/Managing Director, Propellernet.

Give your leaders ongoing support

If your leaders are going to play this important role over and over again, you need to support them on a continuous basis. This not only helps them be better in this role, but it sends the message that this is a key and pivotal part of their role.

At NAHL Group plc, they hold a three-day leadership school for their managers as a way to provide them with support. Key to this program are their values; in fact, the first presentation on day one is about their values. "We do this because we want to re-emphasize to our managers that our values aren't just things that we have to do, but it's how we manage our teams," says Marcus Lamont, Group HR Director.

During the values section of the school, they do exercises to discuss what the values mean to them and how to implement them into how they work and how they lead their teams. This leads to further discussions on how values are used in hiring, recognition and performance management, where again values have a prominent and important role to play.

Read the full play in Chapter 6

The key here is to do what it takes to make your leaders comfortable with being a values-led leader. Help them understand that it's right for the business, for their team, and also for them. For leading in a way that enables their team to make decisions based on values, even when they aren't there, is where the magic of your values really comes alive.

Hold leaders accountable

And finally, it's important to hold your leaders accountable for role-modeling and living your values – never ever let them off the hook for something this important. Going back to the story I shared earlier about Sam, don't let leaders like this continue to lead (and influence) others at your company. In the short-term, they may seem like they are helping your organization, but by the middle to long-term, all they are doing is causing problems by creating a disconnect between what your company believes in with your values and how they are leading and acting.

> *Values should not be another "thing" that leaders have to remember in addition to their already hard job. They should be deeply embedded and an intrinsic part of how they do their job, how they make decisions, how they evaluate opportunities and risks, and how they deal with problems."*
>
> **– Glenn Elliott, Tech Entrepreneur & Author.**

Your leaders will set the tone and direction for others to follow, signaling what should and shouldn't be done. If they are not doing this, they are taking their team down the wrong path.

At Halfords, a UK leisure and car accessory retailer, they hold their leaders accountable for living their values, or what they call the "big four", through their "leadership index". This score, which is given to each leader, comes out of their employee engagement survey, and sheds light on how the leader's employees believe they are leading, based on their values. It's used for performance planning, learning and development, and even as an element of the leader's bonus.

"As a leader, the issue is not belief, it's practice," he says. "If I go a month without telling a lie, that is not living a life of integrity. Living a life of integrity is when you tell the truth when it hurts, when it's embarrassing, when you didn't have to," says Kent Thiry, Former Chairman and CEO at DaVita.

TIPS TO PLAY WITH

○ **Make it a non-negotiable**

It's absolutely critical that your leaders understand loud and clear that living and role-modelling your values is a non-negotiable. It is not their choice to do so, it is an expectation for their role, as with your entire workforce. By selecting leaders who understand this, and then supporting and holding them accountable for doing so, this sends a consistent and meaningful message to them.

○ **Help leaders with their journey**

We all know how challenging the role of a leader is, so do whatever you can to support them on their values journey. Do whatever it takes to support them in understanding the direction and keeping them on track, as it will be a journey, and not a quick fix to help them along the way.

○ **Be brave and let them go**

The final tip is a simple yet difficult tip to follow, one that I've mentioned a few times already in the chapter but needs to be said again, and that is that if/when you find yourself with a leader who after all you've done to support and develop them is not role-modeling your values, be brave and just let them go. Do it for the company, for their team, and for them!

CHAPTER 6

Values in action – the 'plays'

As you can tell by the title of my last book, *Build it; The Rebel Playbook for Employee Engagement*, it was a playbook. It was jam-packed with stories, or what we called plays, that showcased what companies are doing to bring the theory and tips contained in the book to life. They were so loved by readers, and were so helpful to them in their engagement journey, that I've decided to again devote half of my book to this concept of plays, and this act of storytelling.

Here are a few things to keep in mind when reading the plays in this chapter:

1. **Each company is different**

   I know you'll be inspired by what these companies do, but resist the temptation to copy and paste this into what you do at your company. If your strategy and objectives are similar, by all means take inspiration from them, but then make it your own. And then . . . share it with me!

2. **They all do much more**

   To make this book manageable, as I know we all have busy lives, I didn't share everything that each company does when it comes to their values. I say this because I don't want you to think when reading them that this is all they do, for most, if not all of them, do so much more. I've tried to spread the topics between companies, thus sharing different ways to achieve similar objectives.

Plays

So, without further ado, here are the plays. Huge thanks to everyone who let me interview them and share their wonderful and inspirational stories.

ADDISON LEE GROUP

The company

Addison Lee Group is a premium ground transportation company that accommodates both taxi services and parcel deliveries across 123 cities worldwide. It is trusted by more than 10 million passengers per year to deliver exceptional, premium mobility services, globally at scale through its 1,600 employees worldwide.

Their purpose/mission/vision

Addison Lee Group's purpose is about creating exceptional experiences for their passengers and people.

Their values

Addison Lee's five values are:

Delivering excellence through pride and determination

With teamwork we can achieve exceptional results

We respect one another

We hold ourselves accountable

By embracing change we develop and thrive

Building their values

When Addison Lee Group acquired Tristar in 2016, it made them the largest owned private hire vehicle (PHV) fleet in Europe and the US with genuine scale, global reach and strong brand recognition.

They quickly went to work on building the technology to support the acquired business, but just as quickly realized that if they were to continue to be successful and to continue to grow globally, they would also need an anchor point for the growing business, which would be a set of global values.

"As we have grown as a global business, we felt that we needed an anchor point to deliver a consistent global experience. We're operating in a competitive and congested market, and if we want to stand out and deliver exceptional service – what makes us unique – we need something that is clear and distinctive. Our values can help us achieve this." Mat Davies, HR Director.

So, they began an exercise to develop their new set of global values. It began with their leadership team locking themselves away for two days, followed by significant employee input and consultation, resulting in five values which answer the questions – why, what and how they should deliver on their exceptional service standards.

And to ensure that employees clearly understand and then apply the values in their everyday work, they created additional context to take it to that next level. This includes spelling out the shared value, shared belief, attitude, action and outcome.

Here is an example for the Addison Lee Group value of embrace change:

Agreed core to the value delivery

Attitude
- Communicative
- Inspiring
- Partnership
- Innovation
- Enthusiasm

Action
- Take time to understand what's changing and how we need to move forward.
- Seek out what's not working, think ahead and offer new ideas.
- Work with others to seek solutions and improvements.

Outcome
- Change is seen as an opportunity not a failure.
- Personal and professional opportunity to develop.
- Everyone understands the importance of the change.
- All colleagues feel empowered to put forward ideas and get involved.

We believe that change is an opportunity and through transformation and sustainable improvement we will thrive.

Bringing their values out to play

Since launching their new global values in April 2019, they've been on a journey to embed them in how they hire, develop, recognize and manage their people, as well as how they run their growing global business. "Our values are at the heart of our business; they are the eternal truths of how we operate," says Davies.

This is challenging to do in any business, but when a large percentage of your workforce are independent or affiliate workers, it makes it that next level of challenging. For example, how do you ensure that a driver brought in for a job in L.A. delivers the same experience, based on the same standards, as a permanent driver in London?

Addison Lee Group does this by having in place a robust selection process for managing their global affiliates. This ensures that partners around the world know what is expected when they select drivers on behalf of Addison Lee Group, and thus only bring in suppliers that can deliver the passenger experience that their customers have come to expect and trust, irrespective of where they are in the world.

"Having a set of values is much more than putting up posters in offices about what we believe in," says Davies. "It is about changing the way we do things on a fundamental and sustainable basis. It's about creating the conditions for our colleagues to do brilliant work every day and to deliver an exceptional experience for our passengers across the globe."

ATLASSIAN

The company

Atlassian is an enterprise software company that develops products for software developers, project managers, and content management. From medicine and space travel, to disaster response and pizza deliveries, their products help teams all over the planet advance humanity through the power of software. They have over 150,000 customers, with 4,000 employees located in 9 countries servicing their needs.

Their purpose/mission/vision

Atlassian's mission is to help unleash the potential of every team.

Their values

Atlassian's five values are:

Atlassian Values

They guide what we do, why we create, and who we hire.

| Open company, no bullshit | Play, as a team | Build with heart & balance | Be the change you seek | Don't #@!% the customer |

Discovering their values

Atlassian's values came about "based on pain", says Dominic Price, Work Futurist at Atlassian. He explained that as the business grew, and the two founders could no longer interview each and every final candidate, mistakes were being made in hiring since there were no values to help and guide them to the right decisions based on a cultural fit.

So, they used an approach they had heard about, which is to ask yourself "If I could only take ten of my employees to the moon to start up the company, who would they be?", and brought these ten employees together to help create their values.

The result was the development of their five values. In addition to these, there is a sixth unwritten value, which is 'Seek first to understand'. It is something which has become more important to the business as they scale, so is talked about frequently, but at this point, they see it more being implicit in how they all work together. But you never know, maybe one day it will be added.

Bringing their values out to play

"Our values in some ways are an attempt to hire the types of people with the right attributes – fundamental base attributes of how they treat the world, other people and customers." – Mike Cannon-Brookes, Co-Founder/Co-CEO

Hiring

Atlassian began formally interviewing against their values about four years ago, when they found that this was not consistently being done across the business. They wanted to ensure that every new hire was, as Dominic explained, "a values fit and a culture add", which is absolutely critical to the success of their business.

"We don't run a command and control business, but one that is based on empowerment, so it's critical that each and every employee understands the values to make the right decisions for the business. If you do run a command and control business, don't bother with values, you can micro-manage instead." – Dominic Price, Work Futurist

To ensure that the interviewer is not swayed with technical biases, overlooking values in favor of the best technical candidate, they have an independent team who conduct the values interviews. They ask questions such as: What is your favorite of the Atlassian values? Why is it your favorite? How do you use it in your personal and work life?'. They dig deep into the meaning behind the words, making sure that the values fit is right from the start.

Performance management

Another change that Atlassian has made recently is to integrate their values into performance reviews. In order to create a more holistic view, helping employees understand how their work connects to the bigger picture and to each other, there are three equally weighted components which employees are assessed against:

1. **Expectations of the role.**
   This component typically measures whether the employee has fulfilled the expectations of the role, focuses on the right work that delivers against strategy, and contributes quality work that meaningfully impacts customers. Atlassian has expanded this definition to consider whether an employee has gone above and beyond by identifying gaps in plans and helpful to course-correct, taking on stretch assignments to grow their skillset, and inspire others to greater levels of performance.

2. **Contribution to the team.**
   This component looks at an employee's contribution to the team, linking directly back to Atlassian's value of 'play, as a team'. It measures the degree to which the employee seeks opportunities to elevate their teammates' impact and overall team performance, takes a team-view when solving problems, and fosters an environment of trust and belonging.

3. Demonstration of company values.

The final element looks at how employees demonstrate their company values throughout the year. "We collectively strive to live by the values, make decisions that are in line with them, and interact with our customers and each other according to them. Why wouldn't we then bring values into our performance assessments? And it's not just a one-off instance or a focus on a single value, it's about consistently living all of the values." Bek Chee, Head of Talent.

"A holistic performance review encourages employees to bring their authentic and whole selves to work. Knowing that you will be measured not only on your skills but also on your contributions to the company culture, or your willingness to support a colleague going through a hard time, makes for much more engaged employees," says Chee.

Atlassian's performance system is also designed to mitigate the cognitive bias that affects a managers' ability to fairly rate each person's performance. Their research showed that by rating values, role, and team contribution separately, they avoid the halo effect where performance in one area unnecessarily influences ratings in other areas. "We were especially conscious to ensure no 'brilliant jerks' were given a high rating," says Chee. They've also implemented audits and interventions into their calibration process to mitigate bias.

This new approach to performance management was rolled out in 2018, over a 12-month test cycle, to ensure that employees and managers could provide feedback on the new reviews, and confirm that it was a fair and actionable assessment for all involved.

"Our employees are already benefiting from this new approach, with early feedback results showing a 10% increase in understanding of how individual performance is being assessed and a 9% increase in feeling that the feedback from the performance review will help employees improve their performance," says Chee.

BLUE LAGOON ICELAND

The company

Home to one of the 25 wonders of the world, Blue Lagoon Iceland has around one million visitors a year who come to experience their world-famous unique spa experiences, a renowned line of skincare made from their unique natural ingredients, and hotels and restaurants that all bring together hospitality and wellness.

Their purpose/mission/vision

The company's mission is to transform natural wonders into unique experiences. Their promise is clear: We Create Memories.

Their values

Blue Lagoon Iceland's three values are:

Building their values

Blue Lagoon Iceland's values were "inspired by the spirit of our people and the emphasis on the unique experience we provide to our guests," says Már Másson, Chief Operating Officer. And it's this experience, both to their people and to their guests, that their three values address, ensuring that each and every employee is clear of the behaviors expected of them as trusted guardians of this natural wonder.

- The value of **We Bring Joy** talks about bringing joy to their customers through memorable experiences as "unforgettable hosts", and at the same time, create memorable experiences for their people.

- The value **We Care** talks about caring for the safety and experiences of their guests, and for the wellbeing of their people.

- The value **We Respect** talks about respecting the environment and the needs of their guests, and respecting the similarities and differences of the 46 different nationalities working there.

"We use our values on an everyday basis from the inside out. Whether it's business or people decisions, we use them in all aspects and at all times," says Másson.

Bringing their values out to play

In hiring

Blue Lagoon Iceland's values are "always in the back of our minds throughout our recruitment process," says Másson. An example is with their trial days, where applicants come in for 1 to 3 days on a trial basis to see if they are right for the job and the job is right for them. It also provides a great opportunity to see the values in action, giving the assessors the opportunity to see whether or not they come naturally and easily to the candidate.

"It's a big investment, but we believe it pays off because it provides a much better opportunity to quickly spot whether the candidate will fit the culture and live our values," says Másson.

In onboarding

Blue Lagoon Iceland have an onboarding program which they call the "create memories program". The key focus of it is to show new employees what's expected of them, and how they are expected to behave in order to deliver on their promise of "We Create Memories" through their three values.

The key to the success of this program is through their presenters and through their storytelling. Instead of being delivered by HR, they bring in presenters from within the business who have varied and numerous experiences, and can share stories and examples of how they have personally lived the values. This approach shows that often it's not just **what is shared**, but **who is sharing it**.

BROWN-FORMAN

The company

Brown-Forman is one of the largest American-owned spirits and wine companies, with brands such as Jack Daniel's, Woodford Reserve, Old Forester, Sonoma Cutrer, and others. Their brands of this publicly traded, family-controlled company are supported by approximately 4,700 employees and sold in more than 170 countries.

Their purpose/mission/vision

Brown-Forman's purpose is to enrich the experience of life by responsibly building beverage alcohol brands that thrive and endure for generations.

Their values

Brown-Forman's five values, which are pulled together by the image of an arrow shooting towards their purpose, are:

ENRICHING LIFE

PURPOSE WE ENRICH THE EXPERIENCE OF LIFE BY RESPONSIBLY BUILDING BEVERAGE ALCOHOL BRANDS THAT THRIVE AND ENDURE FOR GENERATIONS

INTEGRITY
RESPECT
TRUST
TEAMWORK
EXCELLENCE

BE CURIOUS → BE COURAGEOUS → BE COLLABORATIVE → BE CREATIVE → BE A CHAMPION → 150 BUILDING FOREVER

Discovering their values

As Brown-Forman approach their 150-year anniversary, they've decided that although their values will remain the same, it's time to refresh their behaviors of the past decade: be curious, be courageous, be collaborative, be creative and be a champion.

"Our values are everlasting; they are timeless in how we do business and what we stand for. Our behaviors, on the other hand, are what we do and how we act, and we need to make sure that they can take/carry/propel us forward for the next 10 years," says Andrew Constable, Vice President Global People & Organizational Development.

This decision was made for two key reasons. The first is that the business itself continues to become more global, changing from a primarily US business at the turn of the century, to now a truly global business with 60% of their revenue coming from outside of the US. The second is that the external marketplace has changed and will continue to change, and the impact of behaviors on how they will continue to remain competitive should also change.

An example can be seen with their behavior of 'be collaborative'. With the world moving more quickly, businesses and employees are expected to be more agile and be more comfortable with ambiguity, which in some ways is not in line with how they describe and live this behavior. They've recognized that they'll need to adapt it if they want to continue to succeed and grow as a business.

"It's an interesting point in time for our organization, as we seek to compete and win in a changing world, while at the same time being true to our internal values and our behaviors. It's important that we strike the balance between the old and the new, so that we don't lose what's worked well in the past, but dial up some of the new elements for the future," says Constable. "Of course, we won't stop being collaborative, we may just need to do it in different ways or at a different cadence."

They are at the beginning of their journey to refresh their behaviors, with the goal of launching them during the celebration of their anniversary in 2020. It's an important milestone for the company, allowing it to reflect upon its past and providing an opportunity to look forward to continued success. The values of the company will come through in many different communication and engagement elements throughout the year and will no doubt continue to resonate with its employees, the family shareholders and others.

Bringing their values out to play

Brown-Forman's existing values and behaviors are truly embedded and influence how they get things done and how they interact with one another. This foundation will not change as the behaviors are refreshed, as together with their values they are, and will continue to be, a driving force for connecting their employees from around the world with their vision and their purpose, using them to help create an enduring and growing business.

C SPACE

The company

C Space is a Customer Agency that takes a truly 'outside-in' approach to research, consulting and advertising, by integrating customers into the ways their clients work. By bringing stakeholders together around the customer, they create greater clarity and alignment in the actions that will most effectively drive growth for their 200+ clients around the world.

Their purpose/mission/vision

C Space's purpose is to humanize business.

Their values

C Space's nine values are:

i got this	tell it like it is	open up and listen
show the love	find what fascinates	only accept awesome
leave your mark	put we before me	do what scares you

our values

Discovering their values

C Space faced a challenge as many do when coming through a merger, and that is to deal with the unrest caused by times of change and uncertainty. So they did three things: they developed and shared their three-year people plan, they moved to an open and transparent approach to explain and share details relating to their P&L, and finally, they created values to help the business not just crawl out, but move forward in the right direction.

"We were spending a lot of time dealing with 'symptoms' of issues rather than the root cause. These three things we did tried to tackle the root causes, helping people see that we were focused on people (not just profits), being transparent, and then shaping our culture through a set of co-created values," says Phil Burgess, Chief People and Operations Officer.

They worked together to create a set of values that they call 'behaviors' to turnaround their company culture. Before them, when they surveyed their team, only 40% intended to stick around for more than a year and only 56% were proud to work in their London office. Two years after the launch of the values and following a lot of work on their culture, 70% intended to stay more than a year and pride was at 87%. Three years after launch, attrition was reduced from 30% to 17% and they won the MRS Best Place to Work Award.

The creation of C Space's values was done by launching what Burgess calls a 'culture audit'. It involved bringing together employees from different parts of the business in their US and UK offices, using some of the co-creation techniques they use with their clients. Here are some examples:

- **Art from Within** – In this exercise, employees were asked to draw a picture to sum up C Space on its best day and on its worst. This projective technique surfaced feelings and emotions which people might at first find hard to articulate in words.

- **The Drift** – In this exercise, employees were asked to think about the culture at C Space and then imagine it 'drifts' – all the stuff that isn't good about it that gets worse and worse – what this would look like if things gradually degrade. It was a great way of building an urgent platform for the need for change before moving to more uplifting brainstorming about what culture they wanted to build.

- **Clear the Past** – "Before building a vision for what the future could look like, it's important to create a safe space for people to be negative about the past and the present," says Burgess. In this exercise, employees were asked to describe all the stuff that annoyed them about leadership, frustrated them about their colleague's behaviors, and what was toxic about their culture. "Allowing people to get this stuff off their chests enabled people to then move to a more constructive mindset to develop solutions, which in this case were a new set of values and behaviors," says Burgess.

Bringing their values out to play

At C Space, everything they do is framed by their values. From the people they hire to the ways they interact with each other and with clients, to how they celebrate individual achievements, their values are front and center at every stage. As Burgess says, "Our behaviors are so springy, they allow us to do so much with them, help you do little things that gradually and intentionally drive cultural change as our business evolves."

At the time of writing this book, they are at the end of a six-month reframing exercise. According to Burgess, "While our values have served us really well over the past 3-4 years since launch, we were beginning to hear from our people that some of our values were being taken to an extreme. They had a dark side, as well as a positive one. So, we're in the middle of an exercise to reframe our values back into the business to ensure people understand the behaviors they intend to inspire." The newly branded and reinvigorated values that appear on the previous page are part of a re-launch that will be taking place shortly, and I look forward to hearing how they do this in their own unique and awesome way.

Find What Fascinates Me Fund

One of the ways that C Space weave their values into how they operate across their American offices is through their "Find What Fascinates Fund", which directly links to the value of "Find What Fascinates".

In the past, they had a traditional tuition reimbursement benefit, where employees would be reimbursed for formal learning that involved receiving a certificate at the end. Take-up was fine, but they felt employees were also looking for, and needed, more bite-sized learning that was sometimes linked to professional skills but also to more practical ones. So, they augmented and repositioned the benefit under the new values-led name, opening up opportunities for employees to use it in this new way.

As Burgess says, "We designed it to link to our values, and also as a way to encourage our employees to take more control over their development."

To help and inspire employees, in the monthly learning & development newsletter information is shared on things going on in the area and ways that they could use this benefit. So far, employees have used it in interesting, and yes fascinating, ways such as attending a film festival or taking French lessons, helping them build a real culture of learning, which is a big strategic priority for C Space and the business.

Leadership Development

Another initiative based on their values was something Burgess did with the leadership team in their UK office. Based on feedback from the team, leaders were asked to identify which value they were strongest at, and which value they needed to work on. This was then turned into a big framed poster which hung in the office, visible to everyone. "We wanted this to be public, to show the team that our leaders were not only striving to live and role-model our values, but were vulnerable and human, and that it's OK not to be good at everything," says Burgess.

The second part of the initiative involved a leadership team offsite. During this meeting, they spent quality time discussing values, sitting around a campfire and openly and honestly discussing how they felt they were living the values, how they were struggling with them, and areas where they needed some help. "I wanted to drive conversations with leaders about values, for the value of a value is the conversations and actions around them, and not just the words we stick up on the wall," says Burgess.

CHARLES TYRWHITT

The company

Charles Tyrwhitt, which rhymes with 'spirit', is a multi-channel British retailer specializing in men's clothing. The company was founded in 1986 by Nicholas Charles Tyrwhitt Wheeler and currently consists of 41 retail stores and a successful online business.

Their purpose/mission/vision

Charles Tyrwhitt's purpose is to make it easy for men to dress well.

Their values

Charles Tyrwhitt's three values (three BE's) and beliefs (three Be-liefs) that form their three BE-haviors are:

THE BOSS

"I own my work - its a love thing!"

"I innovate to improve - my ideas are smart; my actions profitable; my energy infectious!"

"I celebrate and champion my colleagues - together we win!"

THE CUSTOMER

"I am customer obsessed - I put them at the heart of everything"

"I think like my customer - to surprise and delight them"

"I care for my customer - happy you, happy me!"

THE BEST

"I own my destiny to achieve excellence - the journey has just begun!"

"I look after myself and others - we put the Spirit in Tyrwhitt"

"I am proud and free to be me"

At Charles Tyrwhitt, they believe in the 'power of three'. It begins with their Three Tyrwhitt Truths (essentially their guiding conscience) and continues with their Three BE's (their values). The values (or BE's) consist of three 'BE'-liefs which each have three 'BE'-haviors. Collectively, they exemplify what it takes to 'BE Tyrwhitt' or how they expect their employees (or what they call 'Tyrwhitteers') to go about getting things done.

"We didn't want our values to be dull or too corporate, so we came up with three themes which our employees could easily remember. We have a distinctly quirky way of speaking to our employees, so we expressed these themes in the Tyrwhitt tone of voice to help make them stick." – Sarah Mortimer, Talent Acquisition and Communications Manager.

Bringing their values out to play

Launching values

Charles Tyrwhitt has a purpose 'to make it easy for men to dress well'. This underpins everything they do, so it only made sense that this purpose was incorporated into the launch of their new values in October 2018. They made it easy for their employees to understand and embrace their values by developing and delivering on a comprehensive and impactful plan which all tied into their company purpose.

It began with the launch at the BE Tyrwhitt Conference in London where they brought together 200 people for a day full of inspiration and fun. Here are highlights from the day:

- **Explained the journey** – It began with the senior leadership team (SLT) taking attendees through the journey of how the values were designed, sharing stories and examples of what the values mean to them personally.

- **Read SLT commitments** – The SLT next spoke about their personal commitments to each of the beliefs and behaviors to make them more real and relatable.

- **Small group activities** – Members of the SLT then led activities where the groups talked about how they felt about each value, what excited them about it, and what worried them about it.

- **Addressed concerns** – The SLT then addressed each of the concerns that were raised by the groups, giving everyone time to work through them and ensuring that everyone eventually arrived on the same page. Key concerns were 'snowballed' up to the CEO to address in front of everyone, giving the effect of one consistent view of the BE's and their meaning.

- **Asked for feedback** – Each attendee ended the day by filling out a postcard which asked for their feedback, giving the launch team data to help them understand what actions needed to be taken next.

But it didn't end there, for when employees arrived at work the next day, the values branding had been plastered absolutely everywhere! They were on the walls of the head office and distribution center, in break rooms for store staff, and even on their communications portal, The LINK, for all to immediately see!

The HR team knew that although the initial launch had gone extremely well, if they wanted the values to truly be embedded into the business, they needed to be reinforced and referenced at every opportunity of the employee lifecycle. So, they developed a comprehensive plan for doing just that, using the next year to roll out program after program that aligned with their new BE-liefs.

"BE-ing Tyrwhitt is a big deal for us at Charles Tyrwhitt. Our BE-liefs and BE-haviors set the bar for how we want our people to interact and work together. They are at the heart of everything we do, providing us with a common language, no matter where we are or what we do." – Chris McManus, Chief Talent Officer

Performance management

An example of how Charles Tyrwhitt embedded their values is with their "How to BE" framework, which ensures that employees remember that it's not just about *what* you do, but *how* you do it that matters. This framework is used across different touchpoints such as appraisals, performance management conversations and talent discussions.

The 'how' an employee shows up is measured by the BE values in the same way as the "what" an employee delivers is measured by SMART objectives; that is, they are assessed against four ratings – exceeding, succeeding, progressing, and underperforming. For each of the BE-liefs and BE-haviors, there are clear descriptions of what it looks like to perform at each of the four ratings, helping employees understand what good (and great) looks like, and how they need to develop for each area.

The employee receives a rating for each of the BE-haviors, and then using an algorithm they've built, their overall "how" rating is calculated in the same way as their "what" rating to make it consistent and easy for employees to understand. Both the "how" and the "what" contribute equally to the employee's overall annual performance score, and dictates bonus and promotion potential.

Recognition

Aligning with the BE-havior of 'I celebrate and champion my colleagues – together we win!', and to embed their values more deeply, Charles Tyrwhitt incorporated their new values into their recognition programs. They created values eCards, which are called 'Living our Values' eCards, which were designed using the catching BE branding, and include an eCard for each of the BE-liefs and BE-haviors. By using their recognition portal, anyone at any time can send an eCard, recognizing colleagues for living that specific behavior.

To go along with these, they've created 'Shout Outs from Leadership' eCards, which consist of individually designed eCards for each member of the leadership group. They are designed to reflect something funny, interesting or engaging about each leader. Although they are not directly linked to values, they serve as another way to recognize the behaviors and actions that help the business achieve their purpose, mission and values, whilst also increasing the visibility of the leadership team.

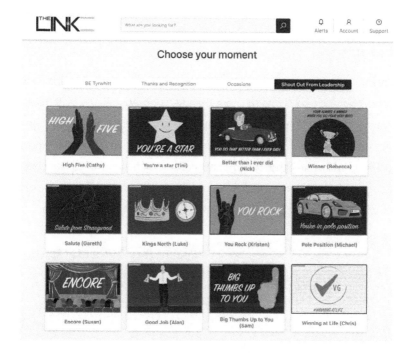

CREDIT UNION AUSTRALIA

The company

CUA is Australia's largest and oldest credit union, offering responsible financial, health and insurance solutions to more than 550,000 Australians. With roots dating back to 1946, CUA has grown and evolved to where it is today, with consolidated assets worth more than $15.7bn and over 1,000 team members. Whilst headquartered in Brisbane, their reach is national via their network of 48 branches. Their geographical spread is also amplified through their mortgage broker channel, with CUA being represented by over 1,500 brokers across Australia.

Their purpose/mission/vision

CUA's vision is to be Australia's mutual leader in growing the financial wellbeing of their 500,000 digitally active members by 2023, and their purpose is members working together through life's changes for mutual good.

Their values

CUA's six key cultural attributes (KCA's) are:

Growth
I proactively work with others to innovate, adapt and grow

Deliver
I deliver outcomes and impact

Challenge
I constructively challenge myself and others

Members
Members are at the heart of everything I do

Genuine
I am genuine and inclusive

Action
I am accountable for results and empowered to take action

Discovering their values

As CUA grew, both through bringing together 171 credit unions and through hiring new team members to support their growth, they recognized a need to set up a culture transformation program for future success and to achieve their strategic goals. "We needed to come together to uncover what makes CUA special and redefine our culture for today and for the future." Tracey Lake, Chief People Officer

So, in October 2017, CUA began this cultural transformation program to introduce changes in cultural health and individual behaviors, aligned to their Vision and Purpose. "We see our values as what we stand for, and our KCAs as the 'rules of the game'. They are front and center in how we work with our members and how we work with each other. It's us at our best," says Lake.

To further support the transformation, 34 Culture Ambassadors were recruited from across the business. CUA invested heavily in this group of team members with intensive 2-day workshops. A key part of their role was, and is, to help create excitement and momentum towards a positive, shared culture.

Bringing their values out to play

Performance management

One way that CUA has ensured team members truly understand the new KCAs is to embed them into their performance management process through the 'Everyday Expectations'. These further align their culture through knowledge, mindset and behaviors from team members through to directors. It also reinforces these behaviors through conversations known as "at our best", which are designed to share examples of positive behaviors and embed the KCAs.

Recognition

Another way CUA has put the spotlight on their KCAs is with their recognition program, which recognises team members for living the KCAs. Three key parts of the program, that are highly transparent and visible are:

1. **eCards** – allow team members to acknowledge one another for living the KCAs. Thanks to the Culture Ambassadors, who've helped market and influence colleagues to embrace the program, it's really taken off, with almost 6,000 eCards being sent throughout the year.

2. **Quarterly awards** – where team members nominate individuals or teams for living the KCAs. All finalists are invited to attend the award ceremony, where a winner and a runner-up are announced, based on stories told about what they've done in line with the KCAs by each of the senior executives.

3. **Annual awards** – the game-changer in the recognition program is the Jack Harvey awards, which are named after CUA's founder. At the Gala Event, previous winners recall what it means to win before the new yearly winner is announced. It's a great way of highlighting once again the behaviors that they've been recognized for and that align with their KCAs.

Together, CUA's recognition program helps to drive KCA behaviors and build the CUA culture into everything team members do.

DAVITA

The company

DaVita is a leading healthcare company and a leading provider of kidney care services in the United States. They provide one-third of the kidney dialysis treatments in the U.S., serving more than 200,000 patients from more than 2,200 facilities. The name DaVita is an adaptation of the Italian phrase "giving life", which is what their 57,000 teammates strive to do for their patients every day.

Their purpose/mission/vision

DaVita's mission is to be the provider, partner and employer of choice.

Their values

DaVita's seven values are:

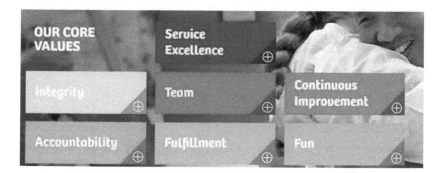

Discovering their values

In 1999, DaVita was in a challenging situation. The company was in rapid decline, and they were on the verge of bankruptcy. Bringing in Kent Thiry as their new CEO, he set out to transform the company and unite the workforce through a mission and values-based approach. Thiry explained to his new team, "We are going to flip the ends and means of the business. We are a community first and a company second."

They used a rigorous approach in creating their new set of values, bringing together more than 600 of the company's leaders from facilities around the U.S. to what they called the 'Phoenix Meeting'. During this meeting, they worked together to come up with their seven new values, which were launched at their first annual national meeting, 'Villagewide'.

Bringing their values out to play

At DaVita, their core values provide them with a set of guidelines to help them fulfill their mission, and for this reason, they are seen and felt throughout the entire employee experience.

One unique and meaningful way they do this is with their "bridge", which is a physical bridge that teammates have the option to cross at any large meeting, such as Villagewide, or office. By doing this, it signifies that they've made a commitment to their mission and values, creating a powerful sense of personal responsibility for them.

"Our values are embedded into the fabric of everything we do. We reinforce them often and in fun ways so that they don't slip away," says Nataliya Wilson, Chief of Staff to the CPO.

Performance Management

At DaVita, they've not only embedded their values into their performance management *process*, they've done so with their performance management *approach*. Led by their value of *continuous improvement*, which focuses on constantly looking at what they do by asking "how can we do this better?", they're piloting a new program called "Elevate", which is based on the concept of a "growth mindset".

> *"In a growth mindset, people believe that their most basic abilities can be developed through dedication and hard work—brains and talent are just the starting point. This view creates a love of learning and a resilience that is essential for great accomplishment."*
>
> **– Carol Dweck –** *"Mindset: The New Psychology of Success"*

This new program moves away from the traditional approach to performance management, removing the annual performance ratings and review meetings, replacing them with more continuous conversations. During these conversations, they discuss what went well, what could be done better, and what the focus is for the next quarter, all aligning with the growth mindset approach and, of course, with their values.

"We've found that with this new approach, the quality of the conversations has improved, it's become less formal and stressful, and it's focused our team on a growth mindset and on our value of continuous improvement," says Wilson.

Learning

Another way that DaVita brings their values to life is in a two-day immersive learning program they have through their Academy. Teammates travel in from all over to attend the event which is held in their headquarters in Denver, Colorado, and have the opportunity to learn about DaVita's distinctive culture and values, study new methods and techniques to improve their personal skills and identify ways to enhance leadership back at their centers or departments.

"At Academy, we strive to provide teammates with valuable, whole-person learning so they can apply these lessons to their lives at home, within our DaVita Village, with our patients, and in our communities," said Dave Hoerman, Chief Wisdom Officer. "We believe that by investing in experiences that help our teammates become their best selves, they will be happier in their lives and more fulfilled at work every day."

During this program, they spend time focusing on their values, providing more color and depth to them by discussing what they mean in more detail to further bring them to life. And with a value of *fun*, they, of course, have developed the program to be delivered in a fun way.

One example is when they cover the value of fun by showing a video of Seattle Fish Market employees, who are famous for laughing, shouting and tossing fish through the air, often over the heads of customers. By sharing this, it brings to life in a real way the value of fun and leads to a more lively and meaningful discussion.

DECATHLON

The company

Decathlon is the world's largest sporting goods retailer with 1,570 stores in 56 countries. It was founded in 1976 by Michel Leclercq, starting with one store in Lille, France. They currently have over 100,000 employees, all committed to sustainably making sports accessible to as many people as possible.

Their purpose/mission/vision

Decathlon's mission is to sustainably bring the power of sport to everyone, everywhere, by designing the best products at the best prices, innovating for quality and performance.

Their values

Decathlon's two values are:

VITALITY

Vitality is an an unusual value in other businesses, it makes us unique since we are entrepreneurial sportspeople! First we act and then we debrief and adjust. Some people are incapacitated when the going gets tough, as Decathlonians we are straight into action when it is difficult. The world is changing and we are changing "a quarter of an hour" ahead. Vitality is also the ability to challenge oneself quickly, be helpful, generous, dynamic, and with smiles...

RESPONSIBILITY

The Decathlete Leader is responsible for the respect of the local laws in their geographic zone. We put in place advice and internal controls to allow us to sleep easily. Decathlonian puts in place the human, economic and environmental indicators required for his/her ambitious project. We are tenacious and find the solutions to reach our goal. We challenge decisions if we do not agree, while respecting each one's role.

Discovering their values

When Decathlon was founded in 1976, they put in place four values. However, in 2015, they decided that it was time to review them again, and made the decision to remove two of them – fraternity and transparency. The three reasons for this were: 1) They wanted to simplify their values; 2) They wanted to put the focus on the two key values, and 3) They felt they could weave the other two values easily and effectively into the final two values. "We prefer to have less values but to live them better, ensuring that everybody in the company embodies them," says Pierre David, Human Resource Leader.

Bringing their values out to play

Recruitment

Throughout the interview process, candidates are asked questions to see how they will embody the values, doing so in a variety of ways. Some are through traditional interviews, asking candidates to share experiences to discover how they do and would embody and live the value, should they come to work at Decathlon.

A less traditional yet effective way is by inviting candidates to recruitment days where they come together to play sports, e.g. soccer, basketball. During these activities, Decathlon assessors are able to interact, exchange and observe behaviors in a less  formal way, being able to see first-hand how they live, and play, based on their values. against their values in a unique and effective way.

Management Training

Another way that Decathlon ensures that their values are built into everything they do is with their new manager training program. All new managers from around the world are brought to their headquarters in France for a three-day program where they live and learn together. Key to this learning is a focus on their values, where they discuss how they live them in their life, in their jobs, and how they can manage against them in their new role.

In addition to the learning they do as a team, they also meet with senior managers, including their Founder, to learn from them. This includes learning about how to manage using their values, and also about their history, so the story of what makes Decathlon special and how the values fit into the legacy and the future. "We want to teach our new managers how to honor the past and build the future," says David.

DELOITTE

The company

Deloitte is a leading global provider of professional services. Over the last 150 years, it has grown in scale and diversity, and currently has around 350,000 employees located in 150 countries and territories. Deloitte Australia has thousands of professionals who collaborate across a network of offices in Australia to provide audit, economics, financial advisory, human capital, tax and technology services.

Their purpose/mission/vision

Deloitte's vision is to be the Standard of Excellence, the first choice of the most sought-after clients and talent. Deloitte's purpose is to make an impact that matters. It is driven by a desire to create positive outcomes for clients, communities and people. Everything Deloitte does is with intent – the intent to make a meaningful difference.

Their values

Deloitte's five values are:

Foster inclusion

Serve with integrity

Take care of each other

Lead the way

Collaborate for measurable impact

Discovering their values

Born out of a desire to deliver on its vision to be the standard of excellence, Deloitte embarked on a project to develop a common set of global values. "We wanted to make sure that regardless of where our clients go, they receive a consistent experience and level of service that is underpinned by our values and behaviors." says Breckon Jones, Head of Performance, Reward, Workforce Analytics & HR Operations.

The project, aptly called "Project Listen", involved listening and collaborating with partners from around the world to create a set of five global shared values. But unlike most companies, the listening didn't end there, as they held further listening sessions to determine if/how local and cultural nuances should be made to better resonate in each market and how the shared values would be deeply embedded in the firm's new continuous performance management framework.

Deloitte Australia stuck with the global shared values, but decided to create their own version of the brand identities for the values, having a real Australian feel to it. For example, they used local images such as a cockatoo (a type of bird native to Australia) and an Aussie barbecue ("the" way to cook food in Australia). "We wanted to put a stamp of our own identity on the values so that they really resonated, and at the same time, not have the normal friction that comes from something which is passed down from 'Corporate'." says Jones.

Bringing their values out to play

Deloitte's shared values are a set of core principles that guide Deloitte's collective behavior. They set the expectations Deloitte has for one another and define how employees, as stewards of Deloitte, should behave. They provide common ground to unite Deloitte across cultures and geographies. And, importantly, they help them to earn the trust and respect of their key stakeholders.

Launching values

To launch their new set of values, the team in Australia brought their 1,000 Partners into Values experience rooms at the 2019 Annual Partners Conference. This immersive experience allowed the Firm's Partners and Leaders to learn about the new values that they and all employees had helped create.

And to bring it all to life, each room was focused on a different value, helping to connect the dots as to what the firm would do to support and align with each value, and what would be expected of employees as well. For example, in the "take care of each other" values room, they shared information about their "Shout Out" recognition program. Along with this, they had recognition postcards each with a shared value on them, where Partners could write a message to a colleague to recognize them for living a value. For the whole session, a live Recognition ticker projected messages of thanks and appreciation through the room.

Performance management

Although the new global values have just been launched, Deloitte has already begun to strategically weave them into how they run their business and how they treat their people. An example is with their new continuous performance management program, which they call "Talkin". This program, as you can tell by the name, is all about talking to one another, checking in and receiving constant coaching, career and performance feedback.

The program assesses performance in two ways which are weighted equally – what employees delivered based on professional objectives, and how they went about achieving those key results through the demonstration of Deloitte's values and behaviors. "It's not enough to just go out and hit targets; at Deloitte, we believe and we measure, it's just as important how our people behave and how they live our shared values whilst making an impact that matters – to our clients and to society," said Jones.

DISHOOM

The company

Dishoom is a UK-based restaurant group that pays loving homage to the Irani cafés that were once part of the fabric of life in Bombay. These cafés broke down barriers by bringing people together over food and drink. Like the old Irani cafés, Dishoom breaks down barriers: in its restaurants, which employ and serve people from all walks of life, at its events, and through charity, donating a meal for every meal – at the time of writing, 7 million meals and counting. The first Dishoom opened in Covent Garden in 2010, and Dishoom now has five restaurants and employs over 900 people.

Their purpose/mission/vision

Dishoom's purpose, or what they call their "Dharma", is to create a world that is full to the brim with the Bombay food and culture they love, a place where a genuine love of people means that anyone and everyone is welcomed with warmth. This is a world where you are always among friends; where differences are celebrated not judged. Above all, it's a world that believes in generous, selfless giving – what they call "Seva".

Their values

Dishoom's two values, or what they call their "Seva" is:

Discovering their values

Dishoom's values are deeply rooted in both how they run their business and in how they treat their team, or what they call "Dishoom-wallas". In the early days these values were spoken about, but not formally documented. When the decision was made to put these in writing to support their growth, it was merely a case of translating those thoughts into words, committing to paper their "Dharma", which is their purpose, and their interpretation of "Seva", which are their core values.

Seva stems from Dishoom's core belief about humanity, a belief that people are at their happiest and best when they are sharing whole-heartedly of themselves and contributing to the world to the best of their abilities.

"Our view is that it's part of human nature to care about making people happy. We all care about this deeply. We call this Seva. Seva means having a big, warm, open heart. And Seva means wanting to be fantastic – first-class – at everything you do. Seva means we don't just serve people, we take them in and look after them to the very best of our ability – guests and team alike," says Andrew O'Callaghan, Head of People.

Together, Dishoom's Dharma and Seva clearly communicate their reason for being and how they, with the support of every member of their team, want to contribute to the world. And although this isn't done in a traditional way, labelling them purpose and values, this aligns clearly with their heritage and identity, with who they are and what makes them special.

Bringing their values out to play

Hiring

Dishoom's concept of Seva is clearly communicated from day one with each potential Dishoom-walla. For O'Callaghan, it's important that each candidate has the opportunity to understand the company's values and decide if the Dishoom world is or isn't the right one for them.

Seva is first communicated with candidates in their invite to interview, at which time candidates quickly hear how Seva translates to the day-to-day guest and team experience. They then participate in interviews and group exercises designed to assess how they currently embody Seva. O'Callaghan says, "One of my favourite questions is 'When was the last time you did something that was entirely selfless?'. I hear so many lovely responses to this, all showing who they genuinely are as a human being, and how they would help bring big-hearted Seva to life with their guests."

Recognition

At Dishoom, Seva is embodied and lived at all levels and through all aspects of the company culture, including their big-hearted approach to team recognition. Recognition is a natural part of how the team work together. It is often delivered in what I'd say is a softer, more personal way, thus aligning with their Seva value of having a big heart.

An example is seen in how the co-founders, Kavi and Shamil Thakrar, recognize and celebrate promotions and long service, doing so by sending handwritten notes and picking up the phone to congratulate team members, delivering recognition in a genuine way.

Formal means of recognition are numerous, but always delivered with this personal touch to show genuine, heartfelt thanks. For example, once a year Dishoom close all their restaurants to throw their annual Family Mela, inviting all Dishoom-wallas, their friends and family, to celebrate the achievements of the year. It is at this family festival that the founders also offer public recognition to the company's rock stars through the annual Seva Awards, which are voted for by the team and recognize those who have best embodied Seva.

Likewise, all Dishoom-wallas who stay with the company for five years are invited to join the co-founders and Executive chef, Naved Nasir, on a trip to Bombay – what Dishoom calls the "Bombay Bootcamp". This once-in-a-lifetime trip is not only a reward for years of selfless service with Dishoom, but a complete immersion in the company's heritage and culture. "In Bombay, the first place we go is Britannia & Co., one of the city's few remaining Irani cafés. Until recently, the café was run by Mr. Kohinoor, a man of legendary kindness who we truly believe to be the embodiment of Seva. Mr. Kohinoor sadly passed away in September 2019, but what he taught us and inspired in us will always remain. Above everything, he proved that the real point of being in hospitality is to throw your entire self, joyfully, into serving," says O'Callaghan. For the longest-serving Dishoom-wallas, this trip leaves them not only enthused about the company, but with a much deeper understanding of the Dishoom world and the world they want to create for their guests, a world with Seva at its heart.

EVENTS DC

The company

Events DC is the face of conventions, sports, entertainment and cultural events in Washington DC, the U.S.'s capital. They leverage the beauty, history and diversity of this unique and powerful city to attract and promote an extensive variety of events, resulting in amazing experiences for residents and visitors alike, and generate economic and community benefits for the city.

Their purpose/mission/vision

Events DC generates economic and community benefits for the residents and businesses of the District of Columbia by creating the premier event experience in the nation's capital, and through the promotion of Washington, DC as a world-class tourist destination.

Their values

Events DC's five values, which they call their 'Strive for Five', are:

Bringing their values out to play

The concept of fully embedding and living your company values is important at any company, but at Events DC, where employees have responsibility for managing complex and sensitive events such as nuclear summits and presidential inaugural balls, it is even more critical. Their values, and the behaviors behind them, need to be front and center in every action and important decision made by employees, whether they're permanent, contract, or employed by third-party service providers, to ensure the safety and satisfaction of each and every customer.

And for this reason, Events DC's approach to their values, their 'Strive for Five', is all about what Misty Johnson Oratokhai, Chief Administration Officer, calls 'hardwiring', making them "a part of everyday conversations, vocabulary, and actions" says Oratokhai. This ensures that nothing is left to chance, hardwiring 'Strive for Five' into each and every HR program, with constant and ongoing physical reminders. "There aren't many places you can go at Events DC where you do not see 'Strive for Five'. Whether it's the values bracelets that employees wear, table toppers scattered around the facilities, or signs like the seven foot one that is outside my door, there's no escaping them" says Oratokhai.

Hiring

The hardwiring of values begins during the hiring process, with values playing a key role. This begins by using interview questions that specifically relate to their values, bringing them into conversations and asking for real-life examples of how these values have been lived in the candidate's life and previous roles. "We believe that values-based questions can help predict the future success of the company and the prospective employee by selecting the right talent" says Oratokhai. And to ensure that managers have the skills required for values-based interviews, they are all trained and all go through role-playing exercises during the company's various management training programs.

They also do this by utilizing selection panels to assess candidates. This helps bring different perspectives to the process, assessing the candidate against the values through a variety of lenses. "By doing this, we can, employ teamwork, one of our core values, to look for red flags that may make the candidate unsuccessful" says Oratokhai.

Onboarding

The process of hardwiring continues with Events DC's onboarding process. The second day of the new hire orientation program is an in-depth indoctrination into Strive for Five'. Although a portion of the training is instructional, training in this area is also collaborative, including a variety of team building activities, thus aligning with their value of teamwork, by getting people who don't know each together to do a deep dive into the values together. One example is a 'Strive for Five' scavenger hunt, where in teams they go on a hunt across the 2.5 million square foot facility, looking for values-related items. Another example involves communicating, another value, but doing so without saying a word. "These activities help employees really get to know each other and learn about our values in an interactive and memorable way" says Oratokhai.

Training

Another example is how Events DC integrates and hardwires their values into their training programs, ranging from customer service, to guest services, to leadership training. Throughout each program, values are spoken about, referred to, and practiced in interactive and meaningful ways. This gives employees constant reminders as to what the values are and what they mean, and at the same time, important time and focus to practice them in a safe and practical way. "Training and development is extremely important in our culture of learning. Our values are weaved into every single training, which places an emphasis on growing highly talented individuals who emulate our core values, resulting in leaders aligned with our overall corporate goals".

GIFFGAFF

The company

giffgaff is a mobile network running as an MVNO (mobile virtual network operator), which was launched in 2009. It was set up as noticeable flaws within the mobile industry created a gap within the market for a mobile network, which operates differently. It is founded on principles of mutuality, low cost, member involvement, collective good, SIM and online only. The business model has proven a success, with the company winning multiple awards.

Their purpose/mission/vision

giffgaff's purpose is to Harness the Power of people. Challenge the established way. Improve it.

Their values

giffgaff's four values are

Discovering their values

As giffgaff grew, they quickly realized that people were key, and more importantly not just more people, but the right people. People with the right attitudes and fundamental core belief that there's a better way to do mobile. The way to do that was to bottle up what they believed and put it on paper. This began with a set of wordy statements, but according to Alastair Gill, Head of People, "giffgaffers just didn't remember them, they weren't sticky enough, and the business couldn't rely on them to help drive the behaviors they needed to help them continue to grow. We realized that they needed to be boiled down to the fundamental truths of what makes a giffgaffer and what we believe."

Gill influenced the leadership team to refine 'the giffgaff way' for more impact and took the next six months to do so in a collaborative way (one core behavior), bringing in the entire workforce, and in a ruthless way, focusing on what behaviors truly make a "great giffgaffer" now and in the future. "Long lists are easy, creativity is all about subtraction," says Gill, which is why they challenged each and every value put forward, 'throwing them all in a funnel', and only having those that defined what made them unique end up in their final four values, with the minimum of descriptions to allow for team and personal interpretation.

Bringing their values out to play

Launching

giffgaff launched the 'giffgaff way' over a six-week period for impact, doing so with activities designed around each value to create excitement, momentum, and encourage them to become habits. Each value was launched by Gill and a member of the leadership team, showing the commitment of the leadership team, and also giving them the opportunity to define it in their own way. This was followed with an activity that brought to life and reinforced the behavior, and an employee pledge where everyone wrote down what the value meant to them on a postcard. This was all part of the plan to embed the four values so that they would become part of people's natural behavior, and not just a poster on the wall or a pointless end-of-year conversation.

Here's how they launched each of their four values:

1. **Collaborative** – they started by sharing famous collaboration teams (e.g. Ben & Jerry's, The All Blacks, JK Rowling and Steve Kloves, etc.) to land the behavior and meaning of the power of collaboration. They then had an activity where teams worked together to build a structure that would prevent an egg from smashing when dropped from a ladder. The idea and the lesson was that the only way to success was to collaborate, as it was timed and teams were large.

2. **Positive** – they started by conducting a gratitude exercise to start people thinking and talking about the concept of positivity and how you are what you think.

3. **Curiosity** – they played the game of 'giffgaff guess who', where employees were given clues about other giffgaffers and had to ask questions about each other in a curious way, showing how being curious helps you get to know each other better.

4. **Gritty** – they talked about how grit is the one defining trait that determines whether you are successful. And, as Gill says, "Not actor John Wayne grit but author Angela grit." They ran an activity where teams had to build houses of cards while loud techno music was played, and people ran around trying to distract them dressed as zoo animals, showing the importance of being gritty and focusing on the task. "Silly, but it landed the behavior required," says Gill.

They kept the momentum and conversations going about their values throughout the six weeks by taking photos during each activity and showing them at the next event. They also distributed postcards for each value on the day it was launched, so that at the end of each session, employees could write exactly what it meant to them and make it their own. Postcards were then put up on posters so that employees could see what each other had written, bringing further meaning to each of the values. Together, this process ensured that values were truly integrated into their language and their individual ways of working.

Learning

giffgaff's values are the anchors of their learning program, being woven into what and how they develop their people. "Our values and behaviors are weaved into learning at giffgaff, but in a non-verbal way. The learning triggers the behavior and feeds into it. We don't say 'now this is gritty' (one of their values), that's for employees to define and make it work for them," said Gill.

An example of this is how giffgaff's approach to learning aligns with their value of curiosity. As Gill says, "We hire curious people, those with a growth mindset, and they need a diet of learning or they'll leave. So, we have to feed that curiosity. It keeps us busy."

For this reason, most of their learning starts with being curious about yourself – who you are, what are your strengths, what's the 'chimp' up to (referring to the Chimp Paradox written about by Dr. Steve Peters), how does the brain work, and how are you different but similar?

Another example aligns with their value of 'collaboration', using Universigaff as a way to bring 50-150 employees together to hear thought-provoking insights from authors, academics, change-makers, etc., collaborating by learning together. It's powerful stuff!

ICC SYDNEY

The company

ICC Sydney is a convention and exhibition center in Sydney, Australia that is dedicated to bringing extraordinary experiences to over 1,300,000 visitors a year, with activities ranging from rock concerts to global summits.

Their purpose/mission/vision

ICC Sydney's vision is to be the best performing convention, exhibition and entertainment centre in the world.

Their values

ICC Sydney's four values which use the acronym ICCS are:

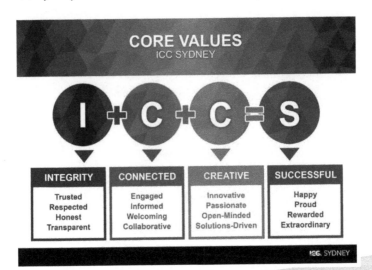

Discovering their values

ICC Sydney built their values early on; in fact, they built them even before their amazing structures were completed and they opened their doors for the first time. Why? Well, according to Mathew Paine, Director of HR, "We needed our values to help us build our workforce, to underpin the way we would recruit, train and manage our team, so it was important that we identify and then look for these behaviors from the start."

Because they had no staff at the outset, the values were developed by the original seven members of the leadership team. However, in 2019, which they call the 'year of refresh', they decided to take a step back and refresh their values to ensure that they still worked two years after their opening. The result was that the values remained the same as they felt they were still relevant, but the words underpinning them were refreshed based on input from their employees. This involved going out to their 1,700 employees, asking them to describe what the values meant to them, and then using this to help develop the new wording.

Bringing their values out to play

Hiring

ICC Sydney calls their interview process "selecting extraordinary talent", which aligns with their Employee Value Proposition (EVP) of "Together we do the extraordinary". Their values are deeply woven into the interview process and into how they train those conducting interviews to make selection decisions. "You may have the best person on paper, but at ICC Sydney we won't hire anyone if they don't show us that they can live our values," says Paine.

One way they do this is through exercises they've developed for their assessment centers, which are used to recruit their casual staff. One such exercise is the "lost at sea" activity, and involves small groups being given a list of 20 items which they have to work together to list in order of survival importance. Although there is no right answer, what they're looking for is how applicants use their values in practice to work together and come up with solutions.

Onboarding

Values also have a starring role in ICC Sydney's onboarding program, taking up a large part of the first day of this two-day program. An example is a group exercise they conduct where small groups are asked to share how they've lived the values in the past, and how they expect to use them in their new role at ICC Sydney.

They prefer this approach over presenting it formally in a PowerPoint presentation, as it makes it more conversational and experiential. This makes it more real, interactive and fun for new hires, giving them the chance to not just see a bunch of words, but start hearing and using them in a work context. Also, since the majority of their staff are operational, working on the convention center floor, sharing boring PowerPoint presentations would quite frankly have them zone out, with no chance of the values being understood and retained.

IIH NORDIC

The company

IIH Nordic is an award-winning digital agency that changes the life of Danish and international businesses through intelligent use of data. With more than 19 years of experience, 50 highly dedicated consultants and a range of services based on the latest technology, customers can expect qualified guidance that supercharges their online performance and aids the realization of their full digital potential through Digital Marketing, Strategy, as well as Data and Insights.

Their purpose/mission/vision

IIH Nordic's mission is to create value through the latest technology and digital knowledge with the help of continuous education and development of intelligent people.

Their values

IIH Nordic's four values are:

1. **Curiosity:** We want to learn, ask questions and ponder the larger perspective of it all. We want to understand the business of our clients, each other, solve issues and tackle problems.
2. **Helpfulness:** We know that helping others is a gratifying act of life: Whether it is a friend, family member, a colleague or a total stranger. It's fundamental to humans and it's what we want to be central to the way we work with each other and with our clients.
3. **Trust:** We work with complex issues and challenging tasks, with a variety of clients. The best way we ensure top performance and personal development is by nurturing a trust-based environment.
4. **Happiness:** We are dedicated to helping each client, partner and team member to have and maintain a positive approach to life.

Discovering their values

IIH Nordic was founded in 2005 by Steen and Henrik with a vision and a mission to break the norms in how they would improve the quality of life for their clients and for their people. Fueled with three values, **Helpfulness, Trust and Happiness**, they set out to achieve this.

But during their 2018 annual strategy meeting, the team felt that these values didn't fully describe who they were 12 years on. As Caroline Dahl Tindborg, HR Specialist, explained, "The company evolves with personalities that come into the company, and we wanted our values to fully describe what an IIH'er is now – how we work and how we interact with the world around us."

So, they worked together to come up with their fourth value, **Curiosity**, to complete the picture of who they were to their clients and to each other. The approach they used to create this new value takes collaboration to the next level. In fact, it almost sounds like an approach used on television to create the grand prize winner of a competition.

They started the competition with teams of five, who were asked to come up with five potential new values. Teams and their values were then combined, and they had to agree upon five out of the ten values. Next, they combined teams, but this time they were tasked with narrowing it down to only two values. And finally, teams were combined one more time, and were told they had to cut it down to only one value. The 'final' involved teams coming together to present their pitch on why their value should be selected, with everyone having a vote, and the value of **Curiosity** being selected as the winner.

Bringing their values out to play

4-day workweek

One of the many examples of how IIH Nordic live their values is through the way they get their work done. Driven by their vision and mission to improve the quality of life, and values centered around **happiness** and **trust**, in January 2017 they put in place a 4-day, 30-hour workweek.

Without a reduction in salary, employees no longer work on Fridays but instead, spend the day on things that increase their quality of life.

"Companies today have a responsibility of prolonging their employees' lives – not shortening them!" – Henrik Stenmann, CEO

What makes this different from other 4-day work weeks is how they put it in place, which is a true reflection of their values, especially that of **curiosity**. They did so by spending 18 months going one-by-one through their processes, picking them apart and streamlining them to make sure they were as efficient as possible so that employees could work smarter and quicker in the new shorter weeks. In total, they made changes in 40 big processes, working together in a curious nature through innovation Fridays to achieve this.

What also makes this different is how they manage Fridays, the day the office is closed, with their Friday 'watch team'. Reflecting their value of **curiosity** along with that of **trust**, they have two employees who are present to answer urgent calls and emails from clients. By taking on this responsibility, they are encouraged to be curious to investigate and understand what teammates are doing to best support clients, and at the same time, trust each other in how they do so.

The results of this bold move have been extremely positive, but interestingly, not completely in the way they had originally intended. Put in place partly to reduce turnover, as a way to stand out from other companies, it has not done this. However, what it has done is to reduce the number of sick days taken, reduce stress, increase employee engagement, and increase revenue, while, at the same time, reflecting their values, showing employees that they are integral to how they work and run the business.

IMPRAISE

The company

Impraise is an HR technology company, based in Amsterdam and New York, that partners with 300+ companies worldwide to develop their people through painless performance reviews, real-time feedback exchange, light-weight check-ins, and goal setting.

Their purpose/mission/vision

Impraise's purpose is to empower people to take ownership of their day-to-day progress and long-term career development.

Their values

Impraise's six values, which they call their 6-pack, are:

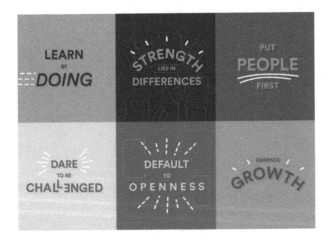

Discovering their values

The creation of Impraise's values was done in a three-step iterative process, with them changing at each step along the way, based on the group's input and feedback. It started with four values, then moved to five, and finally ended up with their 6-pack.

The three steps were:

1. **Think Tank planning** – a group of four from different functions formed a think tank to develop the first draft of four values, basing it on feedback received from their engagement survey and research conducted.

2. **Strategic Leadership discussion** -- the leadership team then provided their feedback on the original four, suggesting changes that ultimately resulted in a fifth value being added.

3. **Test Group discussion** – a diverse group of employees were then brought together to provide input, where they made further changes and added another value which speaks about how work will get done.

When asked why they chose the term 6-pack, Pearson said, "The term 6-pack is often used as a way of describing your abs, which is at your core. And if your core is strong, it supports the rest of your body and helps you perform better, which is exactly what your values can and should do." Anna Pearson, HR Business Partner.

Bringing their values out to play

Impraise's 6-pack was rolled out in these three phases:

1. **Leadership workshop** – a leadership workshop was held to get the buy-in and commitment from the leadership team at the start of the process. In these workshops, they took a deep dive into each behavior, challenging leaders to think of examples of successes and failures, as well as role models of these behaviors throughout the company.

2. **Workshops** – workshops were then conducted with small groups of less than 10 to support the discussion of each behavior – what it meant to them, what they could do to live them, and as with the leadership team, examples of people and situations which would bring it to life.

3. **Official launch** – the 6-pack was launched to the entire company on April 1st, which as we all know is April Fool's Day – love it! To go along with the theme of this day, where you play tricks on people, they created "The Fool 6-Pack", which showed the opposite of the actual behaviors, thus highlighting the undesirable behaviors they no longer wanted to see at the company.

Here are Impraise's 'fool' behaviors – keep in mind that they are NOT their real behaviors:

- **Feedback Postcard** – on the day of the launch, a postcard listing all of the behaviors was placed on each employee's desk which included a personalized handwritten piece of feedback from their team leader with a positive affirmation of how they were living one or more of the behaviors. The great thing about the postcard was that it was the first thing they saw on the day of the launch, and, it's a handy reminder to hold on to and refer to time and time again.

Recognition

One way that Impraise have embedded their new values is with their 6-pack Superhero recognition awards. The way it works is that employees can nominate each other for living the values, along with an example of how the person had upheld the behaviors.

To celebrate the first round of superheroes, the award ceremony took place at the company summer BBQ, where they took advantage of the team all being together. Part of the prize pack included a trophy that represented one of the six values, a handwritten card containing their feedback, and a special 6-pack of beers from around the world (because Strength lies in Differences, one of their values, is about diversity). "It was great to see some genuinely surprised winners and to share some examples of heartfelt gratitude," says Pearson.

And to make sure that all the feedback was shared, every person who was nominated received a message the week following the awards. "It was a bit time-consuming to copy and paste all the feedback together for our nominees, but I wanted to make sure our people knew that they were nominated and the wonderful things their colleagues were saying about them," says Pearson.

INSPIRED VILLAGES

The company

Inspired Villages is an operator and developer of retirement villages in the U.K. for people over the age of 65 who want to enjoy the best years of their lives. The villages are designed around a central facility where people can socialise in restaurants, bars and cafes, together with enjoying state-of-the-art facilities with a focus on their holistic wellbeing.

Their purpose/mission/vision

Inspired Villages' mission is to be recognized as the leading retirement village operator in the world.

Their values

Inspired Villages five values are:

Our values

Our values set us apart and bring us together. They define who we are, what we believe in and how we act. It's down to us to bring them to life every day. With a positive mindset, and in everything we do.

Straightforward and straight-talking

We keep things simple; we don't waffle.

Be inspired

Be an expert in what you do and be an inspiration to those around you. Love what we do and why we do it.

Stronger together

With our residents and each other; we succeed when we work together. There's always time for a cup of tea and a chat to make things better.

Courage

Dream big, make the tough decisions and follow them through. We're not frightened to make mistakes and we learn fast.

Deliver

We keep our promises to deliver the right results. We don't do average.

Discovering their values

When Inspired Villages opened their first retirement village in 2017 with 25 employees, they didn't have values. And at the beginning of 2019, with 6 villages and 260 employees, they still didn't have values. But with a new mission and a goal of growing to 50 villages with 1,000 employees by 2024, they decided that now was the right time to begin their values journey, making sure that by the time they got to their growth goal they had fully embedded values, and didn't have to unpick or change what had been formed over the years.

So, working with their employees, they set out on a journey to discover and design their values. They had a goal of finding ones that would attract employees aligned with their mission and values, deliver a customer experience in step with them, and work together to meet their growth plans as a values-led business, maintaining its ethos of being part of a big family.

Bringing their values out to play

The new mission and values were rolled out during a two-week road-show in October 2019, holding workshops around the country where employees discussed what the values mean to the business and to them personally. At the same time, they embedded the values in a variety of programs, from recruitment to learning to recognition.

"Although we've just launched our values, we've already seen the difference they're making. Our employees now have something to 'hang their hat on', really getting and understanding why they're here, and how they can support the mission of the business through our values" – Lawrence Cramer, People & Culture Director.

Hiring

To ensure that their new values are a key part of the hiring process, Inspired Villages have made changes in the process in two ways. The first is that they've updated all of their role profiles (job descriptions), having them start out by listing which values-led behaviors are required for the role, and then getting into the more technical requirements. This sends a strong message to candidates from the start that values are just as important as the technical skills required, and at the same time, letting candidates decide if it's the right company for them.

The other change is that all interviews and decisions are now made using their new values, so values-based interviews and values-based decisions are taking place. And to ensure that managers have the skills and confidence to do this, they've taken all line managers through training, making sure that this new process can be consistently followed.

Inspired Villages believes that this is critical for helping them achieve their mission, for as Cramer says, "You can train people to be good at their jobs, but to meet our objectives as a business we need to hire the right people and have the right culture. We follow the ABC approach, hiring people with the right attitude, behaviors (through our values) and commitment to developing themselves and the business."

Learning

Inspired Villages have also embedded their values into their two leadership development programs, setting the expectation and commitment that leaders will role-model their new values. They are so committed to this happening, that they've told their workforce to challenge the business if they don't see leaders living the values.

The first program is for their Board of Directors, and the second they call the 'Future Leaders' program which, in partnership with Leicester University, is run for their leaders of the future. Both programs have strong values-led elements, ensuring that current and future leaders have the right attitude and skills to live and role-model their values as they grow within the organization.

"Since launching our new mission and values, we've begun an exciting journey to make a real difference to people's lives – for our employees and for our residents. This can only happen if we work together to bring our values to life, and this begins with our leaders. We're counting on them to role-model how these words translate into actions, and the difference they can make on each other, our residents and our business." – Jamie Bunce, CEO.

KIDZANIA LONDON

The company

KidZania London is an indoor city designed for children aged 4-14 to explore a range of roles and activities, getting a chance to participate and gain insight into some real-life roles, connected to real-life brands.

Their purpose/mission/vision

KidZania's purpose is to ignite the hearts and minds of kids everywhere by empowering them to make the world a better place.

Their values

KidZania's six values, which are joined together by a tagline of 'Fuelled by Fun' are:

Bringing their values out to play

Communicating

At KidZania London, they don't just communicate their values by putting them up on a wall, although their values wall is spectacular, they communicate (and reinforce) them over and over again in many engaging ways.

Here are a few examples of how they do this:

- **Value icons** – when the values were developed in June 2018, the first thing they did was brief their Graphic Designer within the marketing team to develop unique icons for each of the six values. These icons are great at creating an easily recognizable identity which they use over and over again in everything they do.

- **ID cards** – another simple yet effective way they communicate their values is on the back of employee ID cards which employees wear around their necks. Since most employees are out and about with their customers, this ensures that values are always present and literally near and dear to their hearts.

- **Weekly briefings** – to create an even deeper understanding of the values, a different one is promoted at their weekly briefings. And to go along with their tagline of 'fuelled by fun', they don't just talk about them, but have a fun activity to help bring it to life.

- **HR communications** – the HR team have created templates with each of their values at the bottom. They use these each time they communicate with employees, selecting the one(s) that is most relevant, using it as an opportunity to create a connection and raise awareness.

"We take the opportunity every time we communicate to make the link back to our values. The more we demonstrate through the behaviors of the company, the more we can show that they are real and true to the business and to our employees," says Martin Green, Head of Human Resources.

Recognition

KidZania London links employee recognition directly to their values, using it as a way to reinforce and reward living them. To do this, they created values badges for each of the six values, along with a very special 'Fuelled by Fun' badge, which can only be awarded when an employee has received each of the six values awards. These badges have the values icons on them, and once awarded, are proudly pinned on the lanyard that employees wear around their necks for all to see.

Badges can be awarded in two ways – first, through the employee of the month nomination process, where any employee can nominate a peer for living the values. Second, by a member of the management team, who at any time can recognize an employee for a values-related behavior. Together, this ensures that living the values is recognized, celebrated and is visible in a frequent and meaningful way.

When asked how he felt about receiving a values badge, an employee said "I feel very proud. In a job as intense as ours, having your managers believe in you and have the evidence to wear around your neck helps you to do your best each day."

Another way KidZania recognize and celebrate delivering on the values is with the monthly 'fuelled by fun' team award. This award recognizes teams for collaborating and delivering against the values, with the winning team receiving a trophy and a photo which goes up on the values wall.

Suggestion program

The latest way that KidZania have used their values is with their employee suggestion program. Instead of rolling out a standalone program, they relate it back to their value of **no limits – we aspire for more** by calling it their "No Limits" new idea and suggestion program.

By doing this, they once again connect their values back to how they communicate and work together.

KP SNACKS

The company

KP Snacks is one of the fastest-growing snack businesses in the UK and second largest in the market. They manufacture some of the most iconic British brands including KP, McCoy's, Hula-Hoops, Butterkist, Pom-Bear and recently acquired the premium brand Tyrrells and lifestyle brand, popchips. They employ over 2,000 colleagues across seven factories around the UK and their contemporary head office.

Their purpose/mission/vision

KP Snacks has a vision to be the UK's favorite snack company, delivering sustainable organic and share growth, complementary own-label partnerships and strategic acquisitions, for generations to come!

Their values

KP Snacks' four values are:

Discovering their values

Deciding if or when to change your values is often a difficult decision. But with KP Snacks, it was actually quite an easy one as they had just been sold by one company, United Biscuits (now Pladis) and bought by another, Intersnack, a family-owned German business, and as a result were bringing in a new CEO and leadership team, and were trying to find their new identity.

"We wanted to distance ourselves from United Biscuits (the previous holding company) and write a new chapter for our business and for our people." – Johanna Dickinson, HR Director.

KP Snacks used a bottom-up approach to developing their new set of values, conducting focus groups across all sites and functions and forming a cross-functional steering team to pull them together. As one employee says on their company website, "In my mind, what makes KP's values & behaviors so special is that they're genuinely lived and breathed. The fact that they were built from the bottom-up, by the people in our business, for the people in our business, is so powerful."

Bringing their values out to play

With champions

One of the ways that KP Snacks ensures that their values are heard and lived throughout the company is through their 'V&B Champions' (Values & Behaviors Champions). Together they work to embed their values and behaviors into every part of their business, at every site, every day, beating the drum so that all employees can hear (and live) them.

The original group of employees were called 'change agents', as they were put in place during a period of business transformation. However, the first thing the group asked for was to change the name to 'V&B champions', which better highlighted what their purpose was and that it was not about enforcement.

"We originally thought that we'd only need the group for a few years to keep our values alive, front and center in our employees' minds. However, we've found that they continue to be helpful in keeping the quality of dialogue happening in the right way and to help us through change." – Johanna Dickinson, HR Director.

KP Snacks does a fantastic job of using their champions. Here are a few ways that they do this:

- **Personal commitments** – it starts with the 'champions deal', with each champion creating a personal commitment or pledge of what they are going to get out of being a champion and what they are going to give back by being one. This ensures that there's substance behind their work, and it's not just a fun group to be a part of and get a free t-shirt!

- **Buddies** – each champion is given another champion as their buddy. The buddy is from another site, to share best practices and provide extra support and nudges to help them be their best in their role. The steering group also take a buddy site to work with, which provides a connection to the champions beyond the site leadership team to help raise their profile and the importance of V&Bs.

- **Quarterly calls** – each quarter, the steering group host a huge conference call with one to two champions from each site and function to share their updates and ideas, discuss upcoming initiatives, and discuss what support they may need. "These calls are incredibly inspiring – it's so moving when champions, who have never spoken on a conference call before, have the courage to do their site update for the quarter," says Dickinson.

- **Annual meeting** – each year, the champions are brought together for a day focused on their values. It is a combination of development, networking, and of course, some fun activities. This has proven to be a great way to acknowledge the team for their hard work, but also give them additional tools to go back and improve how they perform as a champion. They have invited external speakers (Mark Foster, world champion swimmer and GB Women's Hockey captain, Alex Danson) as well as internal guest speakers, including the CEO, to provide stimulus and recognition.

The V&B champions are so much a part of their values that on the back of the folder they created to hold all of their wonderful documents relating to their values it says "Baked by the V&B team". This shows the important principle that has been key from the very beginning, which is that the culture that has been developed and the tools that enable it to grow have been created by the KP team for the KP team.

Recognition

KP Snacks also bakes their values into their recognition program, which has values at their core. And while this has never changed, what has is the program itself, evolving as the business has changed and as recognition has caught on throughout the business and the workforce.

Here's how the program has evolved from simple notes used by one team, to a fully online recognition program that's used across the business:

1. **Handwritten notes** – it all began with handwritten notes which the Marketing team in head office started using when the new values were launched. They'd write each other notes which they'd put on each other's desks to celebrate each other living the values. So, when the V&B champion for Marketing shared this great idea with the rest of the V&B team, they decided to create something to be used for the entire head office.

2. **Call out cards** – the team then developed 'Call out cards', which are postcards used across the entire head office to recognize, or call out, someone living a value. Colleagues would write each other postcards, put them in a post box in the office, and then they were handed out to recipients once a week. Some of the locations took it a step further and created a call out wall, showcasing the cards for everyone to see.

   The team decided that this wasn't enough, that they wanted more so that everyone would be able to see, and celebrate, those being recognized.

3. **Feel Good Friday** – the team then put in place the practice of 'Feel Good Friday'. In a weekly email, they'd share the names of all recognition postcard recipients, creating a more visible way for everyone to share in these recognition moments. But as the postcards and Friday emails caught on at head office and factories, they found that they needed something more efficient.

4. **Google form** – the team then developed a Google form that could be used in addition as a way to recognize colleagues between locations. However, as the number of recognition moments increased, they realized that they needed something more robust.

5. **Online eCards** – the team then put in place an online recognition program, to replace the form, that is now used across the entire business. Employees can now recognize one another by sending values-based eCards, supporting the strong recognition culture that exists in the business today and in the future.

"We have completely evolved recognition and what we recognize. We used to give lavish prizes to a few people who had achieved something over and above expectations. Now we have a system that encourages instant, everyday recognition that reaches so many more people, and by linking it to our values and behaviors, we have achieved many more amazing results for the business," says Dickinson.

LEGO GROUP

The company

The LEGO Group is a privately held, family-owned company, headquartered in Billund, which has a global presence. Founded in 1932 by Ole Kirk Kristiansen, and based on the iconic LEGO® brick, it has grown to become one of the world's leading brands within play materials.

Their purpose/mission/vision

LEGO Group's mission is to inspire and develop the builders of tomorrow, and their vision is to be a global force for establishing and innovating Learning-through-Play.

Their values

LEGO Group's six values, along with the other pieces of the LEGO Group brand framework, are:

Belief	Children are our role models			
Mission	Inspire and develop the builders of tomorrow			
Vision	A global force for establishing and innovating Learning-through-Play			
Idea	System-in-Play			
Values	Imagination — Creativity — Fun — Learning — Caring — Quality			
Promises	Play Promise Joy of building Pride of creation	Partner Promise Mutual value creation	Planet Promise Positive impact	People Promise Succeed together
Spirit	Only the best is good enough			

© 2019

Discovering their values

When LEGO Group's former CEO Jørgen Vig Knudstorp joined the company, he was tasked with helping the business recover from a challenging time. In order to deliver on this, he felt they needed to do an exercise to put in words what they had done right, and what made them special since they first began making wooden toys in 1932.

"We wanted to boil it down to one piece of paper what was really essential to the company." – Troels Wendelbo, Senior HR Director.

This would help the business recover, stay on track, and deal with the increasing global workforce. As Wendelbo says, "We wanted to make sure that they made sense to our people in headquarters in Denmark, as well as a factory worker in Mexico and a store employee in China."

The result was their four promises, which are a translation of their mission, vision and values in what it means in their four "experiences". They include a Play Promise (towards their consumers), a Partner Promise (towards everyone who collaborates with them, from Warner Brothers to Walmart to UNICEF), a Planet Promise (towards society and future generations) and a People Promise (towards their employees).

Their People Promise, which is "Succeed together", is supported by six values that together define why people should choose and commit the best of themselves to the organization, clarifies the 'give' and the 'get' of the employee relationship, and provides a common point of reference for employees to live each and every day.

Here are examples of how the values were carefully selected to fit together, just like a LEGO Brick masterpiece:

1. To some, their values of **imagination** and **creativity** may seem very similar, but at the LEGO Group, they are different but complementary. In the same way that children play with the LEGO pieces using both imagination and creativity, they wanted their employees to look at a situation from these two perspectives.

2. The value of responsibility was re-worded to **caring** later in the formulation process. This was deliberately done as a way to use more

authentic and warm language to capture the real and underlying meaning, rather than sticking with a value that was safer and would not drive the behaviors that were genuinely important to the business.

3. The final value of **learning** was added as a direct request by the owner family, wanting to emphasize the ethos of helping children learn through play and encourage the same behavior for their people.

Bringing their values out to play

Hiring

The LEGO Group constantly strives to live up to their motto, "Only the best is good enough", whether that's through their products, their services or their people. From a people perspective, this begins with the recruitment process, getting the best people for the company in the door, and doing so by a values-led approach and process.

This was evident as I interviewed Eunice Clements-Tweedie, who recently joined LEGO Group as their new Global Head of Talent Acquisition. She shared her personal experience, bringing to life in a very real way how they use their values in hiring in a very unique and effective way.

"Values were not directly spoken about during the hiring process, but were signaled to often in very subtle and authentic ways," says Clements-Tweedie. This approach aligns with who they are as a company and, back to their Danish heritage, their culture. As Clements-Tweedie, who is Italian, says, "We don't feel the need to dial things up, putting values all over the place on the walls, but instead infuse and imply them in a very humble and understated way." This shows the importance of being true to who you are, and doing things in your own way.

And speaking of their own way, here are a few examples from Clements-Tweedie's experience. First, before being interviewed, she received a text to wish her luck from the person who is now her boss. Next, as part of the process, she was brought to a room where she was given a bucket full of LEGO and had 20 minutes to create a scene representing the journey of what she would do if she joined the company. And finally, before joining, her boss sent her a 3-page handwritten note to welcome her, along with a LEGO bus kit for her to build to represent the journey they'd be going on together. None of these steps come out and say the values, but all of them are deeply woven into what they've done and what they've said.

MISSGUIDED

The company

Missguided is a global fashion retailer that ships to 180 countries worldwide. Their unique style attracts over 300 million annual website visits to shop from a trend-led collection which sees more than 1,000 new styles drop each week.

Their purpose/mission/vision

Missguided's mission is to empower young women to look and feel confident for every occasion.

Their values

Missguided's four values, or what they call 'Vibes', are:

LOVE LOTS
do everything with passion and pride

DREAM BIG
use ideas and innovation to lead the way

BELIEVE ALWAYS
empower ourselves and others to be their best

WIN TOGETHER
collaborate and win as a team

Building their values

Missguided had a set of commandments which had been created from a brand perspective, and spoke about how they should operate. And while these fit the purpose at the time, they soon realized that if they wanted to achieve their vision and future goals, they would not continue to work. They needed to define what made them special, discovering which behaviors were needed to prepare for their future growth, and at the same time, not lose the authenticity of the brand as they expanded, recruited more colleagues and became multi-channel.

"We wanted to bottle it up before we expanded so that we could put our arms around what made us who we were and translate this into everything we do," says Glenn Grayson, Internal Communications & Engagement Partner.

Instead of starting the process in the boardroom with the leadership team, they decided to start at the heart of the business -with their people. It began with feedback or listening sessions, which they called 'Holla at Us" sessions, named and organized in a way to create excitement as well as a fun and engaging space where employees could be completely open and transparent.

The sessions highlighted four very clear themes – love, empowerment, positivity and fun. And to take these themes to the next level, they ran 'Vibe Weeks' intended to uncover what the words really meant and why they were important to employees and to the business.

Each week centered around one of the four themes, or potential Vibes, and involved talking to employees through interactive, and yes, innovative activities which appealed to different styles and activities. Here's what they did:

- **Week 1: Love –** During this week, they handed out Love Notes along with Loveheart sweets, asking two simple questions: "What are you passionate about?" and "What do you love to do outside of work?" Employees were also asked to write and share one of their greatest loves through "Love Selfies". And finally, they conducted a survey called the "Love-o-meter" to ask employees questions about what they loved to do as part of their day job.

- **Week 2: Positivity** – During this week, they dropped 500 little smileys on employee's desks to not only make employees smile, but to ask the question, "What made you smile last?"

- **Week 3: Fun** – During this week, they dropped sweets on people's desks with the statement, "Show us how you have fun at work," and received some great entries. They also created a giant "Ha-Ha board", which was passed from floor to floor, encouraging employees to write down what makes them laugh at work.

- **Week 4: Empowerment** – During this week, they asked employees "What is your biggest dream?" and invited them to write their dream on a giant board in the company's online communications portal. They were also asked, "What would you like to find at the end of a rainbow?" which was cleverly attached to rainbow sweets.

From this, four vibes were created along with vibe behaviors, which were then presented to the leadership team for approval. After much debate, the leaders agreed, with one important caveat – each vibe needed to have a new behavior added that would focus employees not on what they did well now, but on what was required for the business to continue to succeed and grow. Deal and done!

Bringing their values out to play

Since launching their values in 2018, Missguided has been on a journey to embed their values into each and every element of the employee experience. They're doing it in a phased approach, one element at a time, doing it in a strategic and innovative way. "We're serious about not just launching and leaving our values, we want to constantly evolve how we use them as we strive to be a values-led business," says Grayson.

They do this by using their vibes as a part of their everyday language and ways of working, making them front and center in everything they do. Whether it's with vibe burgers and vibe cocktails at their 10-year anniversary party, or recognizing against their values, employees have little chance to miss the vibe they create.

"Our Vibes guide our actions, words and thoughts. They bring us together to define what our colleagues have told us is important to them, as well as supporting the future success of Missguided. It's about being authentic; anyone can write a set of Values and frame then on the wall. However, to truly embrace them and drive a culture of empowerment, the design process has to be fully inclusive. Replacing the word Value with Vibe, a word suggested by our colleagues, is a great example of how we listened, and how something can be created with perfect culture and brand synergy; this is a strategy we continue to embed in everything we do." – Tara Barley, Head of People.

MOSL

The company

MOSL was established in 2015 as a not-for-profit company to operate, develop and design the new business water market in England, which opened on 1 April 2017. As the enduring market operator for the open market, MOSL is responsible for the smooth and efficient running of this new and growing business water market, which allows 1.2 million businesses including public sector bodies, charities and not-for-profit organizations in England to choose who supplies their retail water services.

Their purpose/mission/vision

MOSL's vision is to operate a competitive market that benefits end-customers. MOSL's purpose is to provide the infrastructure, information and governance services, effectively and efficiently, to enable the competitive retail water market to operate and evolve.

Their values

MOSL's four values which form the acronym ERIC, are:

Discovering their values

MOSL had a set of values that had been created by Human Resources before the opening of the new business water market in April 2017, but these had never really been bedded down, and not many people even knew they existed. Once they'd hit this great milestone, opening the market on time and on budget, they decided that it was not only time to make a change in the direction of the business through their mission and purpose, but in how they worked through their values.

The business, however, was going through a great deal of change. Not only were they establishing their new direction as enduring market operator, taking on new staff, and running new systems and processes for the first time, they were also moving their office from central London to Southampton, which is 80 miles outside of the city. Some would say that this was a risky time to update your values, but at MOSL they thought it was the perfect time.

"We felt this was precisely the right time to update our values. We wanted to find out the 'real truths' from our colleagues at a time when things weren't particularly running smoothly, but when there were bumps in the road. This would help us get the most honest feedback. It's very easy for companies to shy away from 'anomalies' in team feedback by putting it down to challenges the company or people were experiencing at the time. I think this is some of the most valuable feedback. If you can't learn from these challenges, then when can you learn?" – Lyvia Nabarro, Head of Corporate Affairs and Communications.

So, they brought in an external provider to help them with their 'start from scratch' approach to developing their new set of values. The process began with the provider conducting feedback sessions with colleagues, which helped them create a list of potential values to be discussed and debated in small team meetings. In these meetings, the teams narrowed it down to those that they felt would work best, clustering together those that fit under a common theme or a key word. These were then presented to the senior leadership team to workshop and sign off the final set.

The idea of the acronym ERIC wasn't something that was done intentionally; it actually happened by chance when they were developing their launch video. The video had a robot as the main character, and when they saw him, they realized that the four values could be moved around in order to say ERIC. They decided to name him ERIC, creating a strong image which colleagues could relate to for their new set of values.

Bringing their values out to play

Launching

The new values were launched in two phases.

1. Phase One: My MO

The first part involved launching the new values on their employee communications platform, which they call 'My MO' – meaning my market operator or my modus operandi (MO) – describing their very own way of doing things at MOSL. Here they shared the 'Why are values so important' video which starred ERIC. This short video explained why values are important, and introduced each of the four values to raise awareness and understanding. Here are some of the lines from the video:

> "It's all our responsibility to build our culture and champion our values. Let's live and breathe ours. Together. And be the best Moslers every day!"

2. Phase Two: Values Day

The second part kickstarted with an all-team values day, which was done as a way to further embed the values. It started with groups discussing what the values mean to them personally, to the team, and to the organization. It then moved onto a stop/start/continue exercise, where they discussed what needed to happen (e.g. start, stop and continue) so that the values could be lived each and every day.

It ended with what they called their 'Challenge 100 competition', which involved fun (and silly) activities which indirectly aligned with the values. The challenges included creative tasks, team tasks, solution-seeking tasks and manual building tasks. Teams were awarded 'fun money' based on how successfully they completed each task, and at the end, the team with the most money won the competition.

As Nabarro says, "It was great to see the whole team so invested in shaping the organization for the better and suggesting real and tangible ways for us to live our values." And to validate this, as one MOSLER shared with the team, "It was good to have an opportunity to reflect on the values with people from different teams, and to hear how the senior leadership team perceive them. It was nice, as well, to get to know colleagues better in a relaxed and enjoyable environment. We reconnected as an organization for a time and that was really beneficial."

NAHL GROUP PLC

The company

NAHL Group plc is an umbrella group of five businesses (National Accident Helpline (NAH), National Accident Law (NAL) Bush and Co (Bush), Fitzalan Partners (FP) and Searches UK (Searches) working across 3 divisions with offices across the UK.

Their purpose/mission/vision

The Group's vision is to become the leading provider in our chosen consumer legal services markets, and its mission is to provide exceptional service to our consumers by being outstanding in everything we do.

Their values

NAHL Group plc's four values are:

Discovering their values

NAHL Group plc created their values in 2014 when the company went public. But it wasn't until 2017, when the values went through a refocus, that they really started to weave them into everything they did as a business, having them sit at the very heart of who they are and what they do.

"Our values have become part of our conversational language. They're completely woven into how we make decisions and get things done. They're in the atmosphere, in the oxygen that we breathe every day. It's incredibly authentic; everyone's on the same page," says Fiona Furman, Communications Manager.

Since rolling out their four values, an additional one of **trust** has informally been introduced. It underpins and is at the core of the others, driving how they run their business, how they treat their customers, and how they treat their employees.

"We use our values as a way to challenge our ways of thinking and making decisions," says Marcus Lamont, Group HR Director. An example is the elimination of probationary periods, showing that they trust employees from the start, that they are confident in and trust their recruitment process and thus have no need for probationary periods.

Bringing their values out to play

Recognition

In 2018, NAHL Group plc decided to change their recognition program, weaving their values right the way through them from start to finish. The new program includes these individual recognition plans:

1. **eCards** – at any time, employees can send each other eCards based on a variety of greetings as well as for living a value.

2. **Value heroes** – each quarter, employees can send each other one values hero eCard based on a colleague living a value. Recipients can redeem the card at an onsite store, selecting a gift of their choice.

"The store creates a user experience, and is a lovely way to make something intangible tangible. It's great to see people going between offices with a bottle of wine, four-pack of beer or a smelly candle in their hands! It starts a great conversation and amplifies the recognition even more in a really personal way," says Furman.

3. **Value stars** – each quarter, leaders can give employees value stars for living a value at a higher level. Recipients receive money into their account on the business communications and discounts platform, and can choose how they want to spend it.

4. **CEO stars** – each year, the CEO selects the best of the best from winners of the quarterly value stars and heroes, naming one employee for each of the four values. Recipients are awarded £250 to spend on their choice of personal or professional development – anything from time management to piano lessons.

Leadership development

The Group has a three-day leadership school for a number of their managers. Key to this program are their values; in fact, the first presentation on day one is about their values. "We do this because we want to re-emphasize to our managers that our values aren't just things that we have to do, but it's how we manage our teams," says Lamont.

During the values section of the school, they do exercises to discuss what the values mean to them and how to implement them into how they work and how they lead their teams. This leads to further discussions on how values are used in hiring, recognition and performance management, where again values have a prominent and important role to play.

NAV

The company

Nav, a venture-backed FinTech company based in Salt Lake City, Utah, is a free site and app that gives business owners the fastest, easiest and most trust path to financing.

Their purpose/mission/vision

Nav's vision is to connect the small business ecosystem, powering transparency and efficiency for financial decision-making. Their mission is to align financing qualifications, predict needs, and facilitate transactions between data providers, lenders, partners, and small businesses.

Their values

Nav's five values which form the acronym RULIO are:

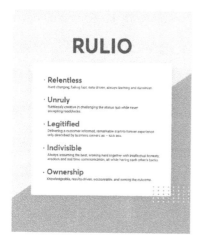

RULIO

· **Relentless**
Hard charging, failing fast, data driven, always learning and darwinian.

· **Unruly**
Ruthlessly creative in challenging the status quo while never accepting roadblocks.

· **Legitified**
Delivering a customer informed, remarkable start-to-forever experience only described by business owners as – kick ass.

· **Indivisible**
Always assuming the best, working hard together with intellectual honesty, wisdom and real time communication, all while having each other's backs.

· **Ownership**
Knowledgeable, results-driven, accountable, and owning the outcome.

Discovering their values

Nav did not set their values from the start, instead waiting to land on their 'product-market fit', which is the product (or products) a company will bring to market. "As a tech company, it's important to set your mission and vision **before** you set your values, as this changes a lot when you're starting out, and needs to be clear to guide the development of your values," says Levi King, CEO & Co-Founder.

Once the mission and vision were established, they set out to create their values, working together to land on five that are held together through the use of the acronym RULIO. Interesting story about the acronym, as it came about a year after the values were launched when an employee saw a pattern in the five values, which were moved around to create this meaningful and memorable acronym.

"A visitor to one of our offices might be confused to hear the word *rulio* tossed around a lot. 'That wasn't very rulio of me,' for example. It's actually an acronym, but it's used so often that it's treated as a regular word, like scuba or taser," says King.

Bringing their values out to play

Nav's values have been in place for the last seven years, with only minor changes being made in some of the words and definitions below the five values. They are used on a daily basis to drive actions and decisions, setting conflict and even preventing it from occurring in the first place.

"The most important part of a company's values isn't the values themselves – those are just words on paper. The manner in which values are embedded into day-to-day practices is key. At Nav, values drive our culture and how we handle all facets of internal and external relations. If we don't stay true to the cornerstones of the business throughout all aspects of the organization, we'll lose who we are and what we set out to be," says King.

Hiring

Nav have always used values as a key part of their recruitment process. However, like many companies, at times they've hired people who have what they call a values 'red flag' as it was a difficult role to fill, or the candidate had such strong technical skills.

However, a few years ago they did an analysis of all the people who had left quickly, so in less than six months, and found that every single one of them had a values red flag. Based on this, they have now incorporated a 'no red flag' policy, so that no candidate can be hired if they have a red flag, making it clear that values are non-negotiable when making hiring decisions.

Another area where Nav use values in talent decisions is when it comes to promoting employees into leadership roles. "Being a leader is not just about your technical skills, it's how you operate in the business, and a key part of this is how you live our values. If you aren't living the values, you are not qualified to be a leader at Nav," says King. For this reason, any promotion is based on both competencies and values, and like hiring decisions, there are no exceptions made in promotional decisions.

Business decisions

"Values have to do with what we hold near and dear to our hearts—the behaviors and attitudes that will define how we treat ourselves and our customers," says King.

This concept of holding values near to our hearts, and then taking it to that next level to use them to guide decision-making is key to the success of any business. At Nav, King says that RULIO has been helpful in achieving this, and shared a story to illustrate it in action.

A junior employee was faced with a challenging situation. They had one of their larger business partners asking them to do something that was out of synch with RULIO. Instead of either agreeing or coming to their manager for advice, they instinctively knew that it was wrong, and told the business partner that they could not do it. "It was such a proud moment for me that our values guided this employee to have the confidence to do the right thing, to just do it," says King.

OTSUKA

The company

Otsuka is a global pharmaceutical company, first established in Japan. The European business's 500 employees focus their passion and energy on ensuring that patients in Europe have access to Otsuka's innovative products in their key therapy areas of mental health, nephrology and oncology.

Their purpose/mission/vision

Otsuka – people creating new products for better health worldwide.

Their values

Otsuka's five values are:

ONE OTSUKA

Our commitments to patients, partners & each other.
Built by Otsuka-people.

INTEGRITY   COMPASSION   COLLABORATION   EXCELLENCE   CREATIVITY

Discovering their values

Otsuka's values were created as a way to bring together their multiple businesses across Europe, using them as both a business and people tool. According to Bethany Mullet, HR Project Manager, "We wanted a way to unite our culture across Europe, to improve the way we work together towards our common goals and mission."

In February 2019, they began this project to create this new set of values, doing so in a way which made it loud and clear that they were indeed 'One Otsuka', creating them in a collaborative way. As Mullet explained, "We didn't want our values to be delivered to employees, but instead we wanted them to be created by our employees."

Here's a summary of the approach they followed:

1. **Culture champions** – they started by asking each business to appoint a culture champion, someone who would represent and lead the charge for their business.

2. **Focus groups** – each champion was asked to conduct focus group sessions across their business to obtain feedback from their individual workforces. Templates were created to give ideas as to how to hold these sessions, but they were then left to run them as they felt was best for their business. In total, 20% of their entire workforce participated in these sessions, so a good overall representation.

3. **Version one created** – based on the feedback received as well as existing affiliate material, they created version one of their values.

4. **Stakeholder management** – the next step was stakeholder management, which was critical to them achieving their objectives. For this reason, the draft values were not merely emailed out for review, but they embarked on a road trip to six cities over a period of four weeks to discuss the draft set of values.

In total, there were four versions of the values based on ongoing feedback and collaboration. Did this add to the work and time it took to create their values? Absolutely! Did it create something that achieved their goal of having values that represented and would help create 'One Otsuka'? Again, absolutely! And, by the way, you may have noticed that collaboration is one of their values, which shows the business that this behavior is critical not just for this process, but for all going forward.

Bringing their values out to play

Once the values were created, as we all know there is much work to be done to take it to the next step. To do this, Otsuka decided to give their individual affiliate businesses the freedom to do what was right for them and for their workforce. They did this in these two ways:

1. **Rolling out values** – to roll out the new values, each business decided when and how to do this. They were given tools and support from Bethany, Louise Christian-Barrett (L&D Manager) and the European team to do this, but they had the autonomy to do what they felt would work best for them. This not only ensured that the approach was right, but it integrated many of the behaviors which are a part of the new values.

2. **Embedding the values** – to embed the new values, Bethany and the team created an embedding framework which mapped out the areas which needed to have values embedded into them, and ideas on how they could do this. This again gave the businesses autonomy to do what was right for them, but at the same time, gave them the tools to do so in an effective way.

The work is ongoing in these areas, but so far, they are well on their way to taking their values to that next, that meaningful, step.

PEOPLECARE

The company

Peoplecare is a not-for-profit health insurer located in Australia. For the past 65 years, it's grown to be a leader in providing accessible and affordable health care to over 80,000 members through their 200 employees, or what they call "Peoplecarers".

Their purpose/mission/vision

Peoplecare's core purpose is "personal is best", which centers around a unique customer experience when dealing with health insurance and improving members' access to quality health care and delivering value-added health services.

Their values

Peoplecare's five values, or what they call their "True Loves" are:

Discovering their values

When Peoplecare moved from being a closed fund, meaning they only provided their services to employees in one industry, to an open fund, so open to others, they decided that it was time to take a step back and review their values. As they were moving from a very corporate "blue", they wanted this to be reflected in their values and their branding. "We wanted our values to more accurately represent what Peoplecare is all about, and to make the branding more inviting, colorful and fun with a link to our core purpose," said Maree Morgan-Monk, Head of People, Culture & Capability.

They spent ten months collecting information through a series of interviews with customers and industry stakeholders, and workshops with their Peoplecare employees and managers. The result was their five "True Loves", with the concept linking to the name of the company, showing how they really care about and love their members, doing so by living these values/loves.

Bringing their values out to play

Recognition

Because Peoplecare is all about sharing the love, they removed their short-term incentive program, replacing it with a recognition program in order to share the love in a more meaningful and continuous way. The recognition program is underpinned by their values, and includes two parts. The first is their peer-to-peer eCards, which can be sent through the V.I.P. (Very Important Peoplecarer) system. The second is their MWAH awards, with the name representing the sound you make when you give someone a kiss, and are received for going above and beyond in living their values.

"Our recognition programs really get our Peoplecarers thinking about the values on a daily basis, including behaviors or experiences they have seen that display those five true loves," said Morgan-Monk.

Performance Management

Peoplecare's performance management system, which they call "Personal Best", has a focus on both how employees perform and how they live their values. And since they believe that they are of equal value to the company and to the individual, they are equally weighted. However, a subtle, but important difference is that how they live the values is the first part of the form, making this the first thing that is discussed when it comes to performance.

Leadership Development

The executive team at Peoplecare spent time together exploring what makes Peoplecare leaders special, identifying that unique and special mix of personal, people and business capabilities that they considered critical for the success of the individual, their team, and the business.

The result was the creation of their "Developing Leaders" program. The program lasts a year and is made up of eight modules that are all underpinned by their values. Throughout the program, they bring the values and the key focuses for each module to life through sharing best practice theory and learning from one another. Together this helps them give 100% as a leader, which is one of their values.

PROPELLERNET

The company

Propellernet is a digital marketing agency and globally operating powerhouse in both marketing services and technology products. They've consistently been ranked one of the top ten places to work in the UK and Europe since 2013, often showcased for the way it works by the BBC, the Guardian, The Times, Management Today, Corporate Rebels, the Parliament Trust and the Chamber of Commerce, to name a few.

Their purpose/mission/vision

Propellernet's purpose is to make life better – for our people, our clients, our client's customers, and our community.

Their values

Propellernet's five values:

Discovering their values

Having values was not a priority when Propellernet started their business. "Having fun, cutting deals, signing contracts and generally scrambling around like start-ups do, didn't leave much time to focus on what we stood for." Nikki Gatenby, Owner/Managing Director.

But in 2013, when they heard British rower, Ben Hunt-Davis, speak about the team's journey to win the Olympic gold medal through the use of their vision of 'will it make the boat go faster?', they were inspired to go out and create their own vision.

"We too needed a mantra, a guiding principle, to help us bring our vision to life," says Gatenby. And so, they created the Propellernet vision, which like Hunt-Davis's was a question, asking 'Will it Make Life Better?'. This vision is used to guide their thinking in everything they do – for their clients, customers, community and for their people.

But it didn't end there, for they quickly realized that if their vision was what they were working towards, they needed values to help them get there, driving the company in the right direction as they grew the business.

"Our values help our employees focus on the end goal and inspire them to act in the right way. They also help our company stand out, by setting out what we stand for," says Gatenby.

Bringing their values out to play

"Values are at the heart of our culture at Propellernet, and as we have evolved and grown, they've evolved with us, shaping the way we work. We make them real by hiring people who share them, and by taking every opportunity to reinforce them. We don't make our staff stand on chairs and recite them on a Monday morning (yeuch), but we do expect them to embrace our values and build them into everything they do." Nikki Gatenby, *Superengaged*

Probation discussion

In many companies, completing the probation period is nothing more than a tick the box exercise. But at Propellernet, after the six-month probation has been completed, they use this opportunity as a way to get feedback on how the employee is performing, whether there are any issues, and how employees are living the values compared to how they explained they would during the interview process.

By having these conversations early on, the business ensures that there is clarity around what the values mean and how they should be lived, providing the opportunity to call out if there are any disconnects or misalignments.

Wellbeing

One of Propellernet's five values is 'wellbeing', and it's something they take seriously through a comprehensive and 'fun' (another value) approach to wellbeing. "We value wellbeing because it provides us with the inner strength to fulfill our potential. If our mind and body are healthy, and our relationships are harmonious, we have rock-solid foundations from which to come up with ideas that might just set the world on fire," says Gatenby.

An example is the 'wellbeing check', that happens every six months. The check-in is used as a way to nudge employees to live the value, and also to make sure that they are engaging with the various elements of the wellbeing program. During the check-in, employees are asked these four questions:

- Are you taking your holidays?

- Are you using your Propel days?

- (Employees are given 12 'propel days' a year, with the aim to 'propel themselves forward' with their development and career progression.)

- Are you using your health insurance program?

- Are you taking advantage of your coaching sessions?

  (Propellernet have a coach for people to work with, as well as investing in the team to study for accredited coaching qualifications in cognitive behavioral coaching.)

These are informal conversations that show employees that wellbeing is a priority to the business, and that living the value is key to them as an individual and to the business as a whole.

Dreamball machine

An innovative example of how Propellernet bring their values to life is through their Dreamball machine. A symbol of their commitment to dreams, which aligns with all of their values, this 5ft-high, old-fashioned sweet dispenser is filled with Dreamball capsules which each have an employee's name written on them. Whenever the business hits a target, wins an award, or "just because we feel like it," says Gatenby, they release a Dreamball, and the person whose name pops out gets to have their dream brought to life.

The dreams have been varied, and include ones such as taking their husband to Las Vegas to renew their wedding vows, taking their parent away on their 60th birthday, learning how to scriptwrite, and even helping an employee find their dad.

"It's an experiment; an experiment in the motivation of hearts and minds. The result fuels our commercial engine and gives us the freedom to experiment more," says Gatenby.

PURINA U.K.

The company

Purina U.K. is part of Nestle's global Purina pet care division. Purina believes that pets and people are better together and is committed to helping pets live longer, happier and healthier lives through proper nutrition and care. For over 120 years, Purina has been one of the pioneers in providing nutritious and palatable products made to the highest standards of quality and safety. The Purina portfolio includes many of the best-known and best-loved pet foods including FELIX®, PURINA ONE®, Gourmet® and PURINA PRO PLAN®.

Their purpose/mission/vision

At Purina, they believe pets and people are better together. Here at PURINA®, many of us are pet owners too, so we know first-hand how important pets are in people's lives. We're committed to creating nutritious foods that will keep cats and dogs of all ages happy, healthy and content.

Their values

Purina's four values are:

Discovering their values

When Purina U.K. achieved their 20-year goal of getting their products onto supermarket shelves in the U.K., they entered a new chapter in their long and successful history. They asked themselves, where do we go next and, how do we get there? "We had been extremely successful over the years, but as we looked at the changes happening in the marketplace and what we needed to achieve, we asked ourselves if we should keep doing what we were doing or whether we should disrupt ourselves," said Calum Macrae, Regional Managing Director – UK, Ireland, Netherland and Nordics at Nestlé Purina U.K. & Ireland.

As a business that had repeatedly transformed itself throughout its history, whether through product development or its purpose within the community, the answer was clear. And key to achieving this was taking a Purina interpretation of the "Four Respect" values together with Purina's passion for pets. According to Macrae, "To support our transformation we felt we needed to bring our values to life, starting with our employees and our passion for pets. This would give us the focus to deliver our next chapter and set up for the future to deliver on our purpose."

Purina U.K. shares the values of their parent company, Nestlé, but, being a pet care company, they also bring a unique focus on pets through their value of having a 'Passion for Pets'.

Bringing their values out to play

At Purina, they believe that when people and pets come together, life is better. It's a sentiment that has been part of their businesses throughout time, and it's this belief that is placed at the heart of everything they do and the products they make. So, it should come as no surprise that respect for others (including a passion for pets) is brought to life in many ways, both within the community and within the company. Here are two ways they do this:

1. Pets at Work

The first example is through their "Pets at Work" program, which not only aligns with the value of *visible care*, but is also one of their 10 "Purina in Society Commitments".

"We know that pets have a hugely positive impact on our mental and physical health and wellbeing, but longer working hours, increased on-the-go consumerism and the population moving from rural to a more urban lifestyle can make it

difficult to accommodate pets into 21st-century lives. Our Pets at Work scheme gives all employees the chance to bring their four-legged friends into the office. We hope sharing our experience will inspire other companies to open their doors to dogs too!" says Macrae.

The program is about helping companies become pet-friendly and benefit from their experience to help facilitate this transformation. From dog-friendly signage to dog behavioral assessments, they help companies implement a successful and durable program. And by doing this, they're not only living their value, but with over 50 alliances with companies across Europe, others are helping them bring this value to life each and every time they receive a cuddle, hug or even lick from one of their four-legged friends.

2. Mental Health & Wellness

And it's not just about their customers, or their pets, where this value has been brought to life. For at Purina U.K. they've also made a commitment to improve the support they provide to their employees when it comes to their mental health and wellness, bringing the value of visible care to life in the workplace. "We believe the incredible importance of this subject, and how it is absolutely central to our desire to be a fully inclusive workplace and, in simple terms, the importance of looking out for each other and looking after each other," says Macrae.

1. They've signed the 'Time to Change' pledge, joining over 1,200 organizations in the U.K. in their commitment to change how we think and
   act about mental health in the workplace.
2. All managers in their head office have taken a one-day mental health
   training program through MIND, a mental health charity, and all
   employees have access to a MIND eLearning module.
3. They've put in place a new 24/7 employee assistance program for
   employees and their families to provide support with work and personal matters.
4. They're running Mental Health Awareness weeks where they campaign around specific topics, share stories, and raise awareness to
   start conversations on this important topic.

The wonderful thing about these initiatives is that they were conceived
by their employees, and not at the leadership level. By embracing their
values, taking pride in its intent, they've already made a difference in this
important and often neglected area.

RADIO FLYER

The company

Radio Flyer is an American company, founded in 1917 by Italian immigrant Antonio Pasin, that is known for designing quality products that spark imagination and inspire active play for kids of all ages.

Their purpose/mission/vision

Radio Flyer's mission, which forms the acronym 'RADIO', is:

MISSION
To bring smiles to kids of all ages and to create warm memories that last a lifetime.

By our actions:
Relentless commitment to build a great team.
Awesome kids products that inspire active play.
Deliver breakthrough results.
Improve our world by acting sustainably.
Outstanding Little Red Rule customer service.

Their values

Radio Flyer's six values that form the acronym FLYER, that along with their mission, creatively join together to form the acronym RADIO FLYER are:

VALUES
We follow the **"Little Red Rule:"**
Every time we touch people's lives, they will feel great about Radio Flyer.

Because we live the **Flyer Code**:
FUNomenal Customer Experiences
Live with Integrity
Yes I can
Excellence in Everything
Responsible for Success

Just as Radio Flyer's products fuel the imagination of children, their company values, or what they call the 'Flyer Code', fuel the behaviors of employees, who they call 'Flyers', helping them succeed personally and as a business. They were created 14 years ago, and have been tweaked twice to reframe them so employees can better remember and use them.

And just as any great product is a result of all of its parts, the values work together with their vision, which is **to be the world's most loved children's brand**, and their mission, which is **to bring smiles to kids of all ages and to create warm memories that last a lifetime**.

Bringing their values out to play

Hiring

Radio Flyer use their values throughout the hiring process. It starts with a letter which is sent by their Chief Wagon Officer listing their values, thus giving candidates the opportunity to self-assess and determine whether their personal values align with the company's or not.

"Even before the assessment process, we are putting the values in front of the decision-makers, the candidates, creating a mutual process from the start." – Amy Bastuga, Chief People Officer

The process continues into the interview, with the interviewer asking questions which relate to each value, having the candidate give examples of how they've lived the values in their personal and work life.

And finally, values are woven into the written assignment which each candidate is asked to write and present. They're asked to think through and then present on three successes and one failure, and what they've learned from these.

Together, this ensures that values are the foundation, and the 'star', of the process and of decision-making – for the candidate and for the company.

Onboarding

Values continue to be present, modeled and reinforced throughout Radio Flyer's onboarding and assimilation process. Here are a few examples of how they do this throughout their four-stage process:

1. **Welcome Lunch** – During the welcome lunch, new employees are introduced to those who have won the Little Red Rule, so have been awarded and acknowledged for modeling the values. This provides for a great welcome experience, and connects them with people who set a positive example in living the values.

2. **Wagon U** – A key part of onboarding is 'Wagon U', where there are 10 courses for new employees. The courses, which are taught by an internal faculty consisting of every senior leader on the executive team, give new employees the tools and a shared language to help them live the values.

3. **FUNomenal Customer Experiences**: To bring the value 'FUNomenal customer experiences' to life, new employees shadow the consumer services team and participate in consumer phone calls. This shows them firsthand how the value is lived, translating them from words to actions.

Performance management

Radio Flyer is so committed to their values that it doesn't end once the onboarding process ends, but continues into programs such as performance management. Here, values are equally weighted with results, showing the importance they place on employees being held accountable for not just knowing their values, but actually living them.

"Values are reflected in behaviors, so of course they're used in performance management. The intention is to hold people accountable for their behaviors," says Bastuga.

And if you're wondering how this works, it's because Radio Flyer's values are not 'pink and fluffy' as some values are, but are written in a way that the values, the behaviors, can easily be seen in practice.

"None of our values talk about being nice, but represent behaviors you need to be successful," says Bastuga.

RALPH TRUSTEES LTD

The company

Ralph Trustees Ltd is a family-owned, family-run, independent group of three hotels based in the UK. Under the creative vision of the owners, each property retains a unique personality rooted in its heritage, grounded in their high standards, pride in their 850 employees and a warm welcome to all of their guests.

Their purpose/mission/vision

Ralph Trustees is a small family with a big personality where people and success matter.

Their values

Ralph Trustees' six values are:

Discovering their values

When Daniel and Stuart Levy first started running the business in the mid-1980s, one of the first things they did was create values, something to help them define what they wanted their business and their legacy to be. Zoom ahead to 2019, when the business and the world around them had changed, and they decided it was time that their values changed as well.

The Ralph Trustees' new values were created by involving employees throughout the process, working together to define what they would be. "Our new values are rooted in the old ones, but are snappier and have put more emphasis and energy into the areas which we need to focus on and talk about," says Katy Grêlé, Group HR Director.

Bringing their values out to play

Ralph Trustees launched their values in three phases:

- **To leaders** – they began first with their owners and leaders, bringing them together for a workshop prior to the official launch. They did this as they wanted to spend time with leaders so that they understood the new values, what would be covered during workshops with their teams, and just as importantly, what would be expected of them with respect to owning and living the new values. "We didn't want the values to fall off the cliff when our leaders got busy; we wanted to set them up to become a way to get things done and understand that they are the heart of the business," says Grêlé.

- **To champions** – a diverse team of champions were selected from every business function, and then brought together for the second of the values workshops. During these sessions they went through what would be covered in the workshops as well as what would be expected of them as they led and ran workshops, giving them the confidence and skills to do so.

- **To the workforce** – values workshops were then held across the business, being led by champions along with support from their General Manager and an HR representative. "We had the values champions run the sessions as we didn't want it to be seen as an HR or senior management initiative. We wanted it to be words spoken from colleagues when they heard the new values for the first time," says Grêlé.

The objectives of the workshops were to remind employees of their history, explain why the new values were created, and what they were. They ran them by using a mix of playful exercises and those that dug a bit deeper into the meaning of the values.

Here are a few examples of the workshop exercises:

1. For the value of **warm** – pictures were hung on the walls of things that may make you think of this value. Employees were asked to stand by the picture that spoke to them the most about being warm, and they discussed why and how it related to this value in their job and at the company.

2. For the value of **thoughtful** – employees were asked to write on a Post-it something thoughtful from their hotel – either that had been done to them, they had seen, or they believe the company does in a thoughtful way. These Post-it notes have been put up on permanent thoughtful walls which have been created in staff break rooms to remind employees of the meaning of this value.

3. For the value of **ethical** – employees were given ethics questions such as "what would do if you found money on the floor in a restaurant?". They were then asked to stand by the answer that they agreed with, and as a group, discussed what this meant in respect to their new value.

"Our employees have really liked the interactive and inclusive style of the workshops. They created a fantastic buzz and momentum in the business, and have led to people putting energy around solving some of those issues that had been stopping them moving forward, with a real sense of optimism and ambition for the future," says Grêlé.

Starting the embedding process

Although the values have just been launched, the team at Ralph Trustees have already taken steps to embed their values in the organization so that the education and discussions continue after day one. Here are three examples of how they've done this:

1. **Mini version of workshop** – they created a mini version of the launch workshop to be used during the onboarding process. This ensures that the great work done during the launch workshops continues with new employees.

2. **Values champion meeting** – they pulled together values champions to debrief and learn from the workshops, getting their thoughts on how and when the values could be embedded throughout the organization and how they'd continue to get their buy-in for going forward.

3. **Toolkit for team huddles** – they created a toolkit, to be sent to each department head, having material for a 6-week values campaign to happen two months after the initial launch. The reason for this was to keep the conversations and focus on the values, providing another formal opportunity to do this.

The toolkit contained a different activity to be run for each value for a week. Each activity had a similar structure, but the activities varied, based on the value. An example is that for the value of ambition, they were asked to write on a postcard an ambition they had for their job, their team or the business. The manager held the postcards for three months, and then handed them out again for employees to discuss how they had lived this value.

Ralph Trustees are at the beginning of their values journey, but if what they've done so far is any indication, they are certainly on the right track.

REWARD GATEWAY

The company

Reward Gateway is an employee engagement technology company that supports organizations to attract, engage, and retain their best people through technology solutions for employee recognition, discounts, benefits, surveys and communication. They have 450 employees who support over 1,800 clients globally, and are on a unified mission to Make the World a Better Place to Work.

Their purpose/mission/vision

Reward Gateway's mission is "To make the world a better place to work".

Their values

Reward Gateway's eight values are:

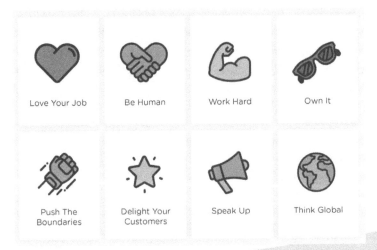

| Love Your Job | Be Human | Work Hard | Own It |
| Push The Boundaries | Delight Your Customers | Speak Up | Think Global |

Bringing their values out to play

Reward Gateway have their values at the heart of everything they do. They sit proudly on their walls, using LEGO models to create a bit of fun and engagement, have a prominent space on their communications portal, create the content for their Culture Book, and are used throughout all areas of the employee experience.

Bringing values together

One of the biggest challenges a company faces when it comes to values is – how do you get employees to remember them, or better yet, how do you get employees to understand what they really mean? If you can't get past this hurdle, you have no chance of them ever being lived!

With eight values and a global workforce, this is exactly the challenge that Reward Gateway faced, and then tackled by creating and using a rocket ship metaphor. The drawing and the story explain how their values link together and support their North Star value of 'delight your customers' that connects to their mission of 'Let's make the world a better place to work'.

rg.co/rocketship

Welcoming your employees with a wow

At Reward Gateway, they introduce their values to new hires in a few different ways. As Robert Hicks, Group HR Director, says, "The more understanding your new hires have of your culture and values, the more likely they'll live them from Day One."

The first way they do this is by spotlighting a new value each day during the onboarding process. This is done via their internal communications system which is called 'boom!', with a deep dive into each value along with examples of how it plays out in their workplace.

Another way is through the use of their welcome box. The contents of the box have been thoroughly planned out to align with the company's purpose, mission, and eight values, and last but not least, to show the RG culture 'in a box'. The box contains eight items, each having a gift tag to name and connect to a value, which includes:

1. **Culture book** (value = Speak up) – to encourage new starters to learn about our culture and values and speak up about what they do and don't like.

2. **Volunteering voucher** (value = Push the boundaries) – to highlight our volunteering benefit and show how we're making a difference and pushing the boundaries.

3. **Book** (value = Own it) – a book for self-development.

4. **Postcards** (value = Think global) – to use to send to RG'ers across the globe.

5. **A pledge** to make the world a better place to work (value = delight your customers) – the commitment to our mission.

6. **Job description** (value = Work hard) – a reminder of what they're here to do.

7. **Water bottle** (value = Love your job) – to represent the RG thirst for knowledge and success.

Recognition

A final example of how Reward Gateway use their values is through their global recognition program, which they call MORE (standing for 'moments of recognition everyday'). The program was designed based on their values, using a global team to ensure that it aligned with their value of 'think global' and delivered on the values of 'push the boundaries' and 'delight the customer' by creating a best-in-class recognition program.

The recognition program consists of four 'layers', all recognizing employees who live the values. And to celebrate recognition moments, and at the same time highlight for others what it looks like to live the values, recognition eCards appear on their recognition portal for all to see and comment on.

Also, the eCards are more than just a simple thank you. Their team follows their model for strategic recognition, where each person who sends an eCard includes the action, connects to the value, and then explains the impact the action made.

"Recognizing against values in a strategic way helps every employee in the company to see what it means to live our values and how to replicate value-based behavior that supports our strategic objectives and overall mission. It also brings our company together building relationships and making everyone feel respected and valued for their work, critical elements to increasing motivation and engagement," says Hicks.

ST JOHN AMBULANCE

The company

St John Ambulance (SJA) is the UK's leading first aid charity. Every year, their 30,000 employees and volunteers provide first aid across 600 locations and teach more than 400,000 people how to save a life through a variety of training programs.

Their purpose/mission/vision

SJA's vision is that everyone who needs it should receive first aid from those around them. No one should suffer for the lack of trained first aiders.

Their values

SJA's five values that form the acronym HEART are:

Discovering their values

A few years ago, SJA decided that their values were old and stale, and therefore they needed something new that would resonate with their 2,000 employees and 28,000 volunteers. So, they put together a team which included employees and volunteers, ensuring that all areas of the organization were represented, and came up with their new set of values.

SJA's values were intended to win and lead the hearts and minds of their workforce, which is challenging in any company, but even more so when 93% of your workforce are volunteers. So, they decided to create an acronym to help with this, using it as a way to create immediate and ongoing meaning, and as a way to help their workforce remember their new values. They went round and round, testing various acronyms with their workforce, and finally landed on HEART, which people absolutely loved.

"We're a healthcare charity and we love a cheesy, health-related acronym!" – Steve Foster – Director of People & Organization.

Bringing their values out to play

The values have really caught on with employees and volunteers alike, and now form the basis of their competency framework, where leadership behaviors are included in their performance and development review process.

"The most powerful thing is how often people will challenge someone or something other by saying, "That's not in line with the HEART values" which far outweighs the values' inclusion in any process or poster." – Steve Foster – Director People & Organization

Re-packaged competencies

SJA had a set of competencies, but once the new values were developed, they decided to take the opportunity to re-package and reframe them.

"We felt it was confusing to have something different for our competencies, so we made the decision to update them to fit under our new HEART framework." – Steve Foster – Director People & Organization.

By doing this, SJA not only created alignment, but used it as a way to integrate their values into the language that would be taking place in conversations about behaviors and competencies.

They developed two sets of competencies, one set for their employees and volunteers, and another set for their leaders. They have the same look and feel to show the alignment, with the leader's competencies having a bit more as they want their leaders to go above and beyond in how they build a culture where everyone can live the values.

Recognition

When the new values were rolled out, a poster was created to showcase the values to employees across their 600 locations. One of the leaders decided to shrink down the poster to postcard size, and use them as a way to recognize his team against the new set of values.

These recognition postcards have caught on so much that the original 2,000 cards quickly disappeared, and an additional 20,000 had to be re-printed.

What's great about these postcards is that they link to the values, again helping them to become a part of their 'normal' language. They also bring a bit of HEART to recognition in that they are handwritten, so have that personal touch, and by sending them to home addresses, employees can share the love with their friends and family members.

Working alongside the postcards is their online notice board, which is where all employees can post recognition messages in a more public way. Together, these recognition programs highlight the values and behaviors that SJA have created to ensure that their vision is delivered through each and every employee and volunteer.

STARRED

The company

Starred is a technology company, based in Amsterdam and London, that is used by over 250 companies worldwide to collect candidate and employee feedback and create a human-first feedback culture.

Their purpose/mission/vision

Starred's mission is to make feedback better for everyone, and their vision is to make Starred the standard for feedback.

Their values

Starred's five values are:

 **Starred**

We make feedback **better for everyone.**

| Work smarter | Building together | Embrace & drive change | Start with the human | Take ownership |

Bringing their values out to play

About a year ago, the team at Starred worked together to define their mission and values, creating ones that truly reflected the culture and ethos of the company. However, a year later, something happened . . .

"I was living in London, busy getting initial traction for us in our new market. I was having regular calls with my team back in the Netherlands to stay connected, but one after another they were getting increasingly vocal about our culture, telling me that they just weren't happy. They were saying that 'Starred isn't Starred anymore, and there were key employees ready to leave. It was time for action!" – Lars van Wieren, Founder & CEO.

The mistake was that although they had created and introduced their values, they had not embedded them. "As well-thought-out as our values were, we weren't living by them," says van Wieren. So, they assembled a team, which they called "S Club 7", and set off to make them visible, alive, and a part of each and every practice and guideline.

Hiring

So important is hiring employees who embody their values, that van Wieren conducts a values-based final interview with each and every candidate.

"The conversation is anchored around our values, and I figure out how well they resonate with the candidate. It's a great way for me to learn about the candidate, and for the candidate to learn about Starred. It's the perfect moment to explain our values, so they don't come as a surprise to them later on," says van Wieren.

Here's an example of the questions asked for the value of 'Start with the human', and how they score it using their feedback tool.

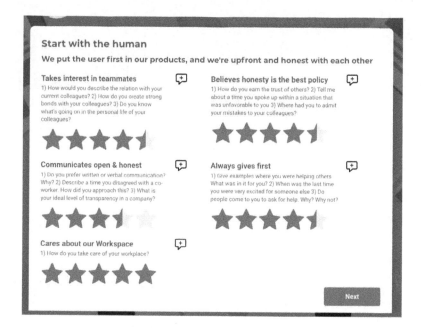

Recognition

Another example of how Starred have embedded their values is with their recognition program. They do it in these three creative ways:

1. **Bi-annual value awards**. Twice a year, employees nominate each other for awards based on their five values. Winners are selected using a clapometer approach, with the person receiving the loudest cheers winning the award. The award, "the ugliest trophy I could find" says van Wieren, sits proudly on the winner's desk until the new winners are announced.

2. **Rotating emojis**. For each value, Starred created a custom rotating emoji to be used to recognize one another on their online communications tool. This works well to create an identity and immediate identification with the values, and sets the tone for recognition messages.

3. **Post its**. And finally, Starred have created a values recognition wall. On it, employee photos appear, and anyone at any point in time can write a values-based recognition message on a Post-it and put it next to the person's photo for all to see.

TRUSTFORD

The company

TrustFord is part of the Ford Retail Group, which is owned by Ford Motor Company. They operate an independent dealer group, selling around 100,000 vehicles each year across the UK, and employ over 3,000 people who work together as part of the TrustFord Family.

Their purpose/mission/vision

TrustFord's purpose is to drive the standard in customer care.

Their values

TrustFord's four values, which they call 'principles', and are part of their PPA are:

Discovering their values

In 2014, TrustFord set a goal of being listed on the 'Sunday Times' 100 Best Places to Work For'. When sitting down to develop their plan, they quickly realized that in order to achieve this, they needed to start with a common language as to what their purpose and ambition was, and how they should behave to get there.

They spent the next 12 months working on this and getting it right, and in 2015 they launched what they call their 'PPA', which defines their purpose, their principles (values), and their ambition, bringing it all together under this easily remembered acronym. And the result; they've been on the Sunday Times list for the last 4 years running!

Bringing their values out to play

TrustFord have worked hard to embed their values into the DNA of their organization, weaving them into their various HR programs and into their language.

"When we put anything out to the business, it aligns with our PPA so that there is a consistent message for our people. I'm a strong believer that if you start using different language, the clarity will get diluted." – Sharon Ashcroft, HR Director.

Hiring

TrustFord recruit against their values in a comprehensive and unique way. They do this by building their values into each step of the recruitment process. An example is the first step of the recruitment process, which is a test that was written by a psychologist, based on their behaviors. A link to the online test is sent to applicants once they apply for a position, and if they pass, they are invited to attend an assessment center, which is the second step of the process.

As Ashcroft says, "As we recruit on behaviors, we need to validate potential colleagues before they arrive to interview to ensure they fit with our values." They feel so strongly about this that if an applicant does not pass the test, they are not allowed to apply for a job with them again.

Onboarding

Another example of how TrustFord use their values is in their onboarding process. All new employees are invited to a two-day residential class at their Academy, where all activities are directly or indirectly based around their PPA.

An example is an exercise they do where employees get into groups to discuss what the PPA means to them in their individual roles, both within the company and with external customers. By doing this, all employees have a clear understanding of what's expected of them, and how they can use the PPA as a guidepost to doing their job to achieve their purpose and ambition.

VALOR HOSPITALITY

The company

Valor Hospitality manages over 50 hotels around the globe, branded under all of the main brands – Hilton, Marriott and IHG.

Their purpose/mission/vision

Valor Hospitality's purpose is to establish Valor Hospitality Europe as a respected, successful and dynamic management company. Valor will be known for having highly engaged people delivering great levels of hospitality with commercial expertise second to none.

Their values

Valor Hospitality's five values that form the acronym PRIDE are:

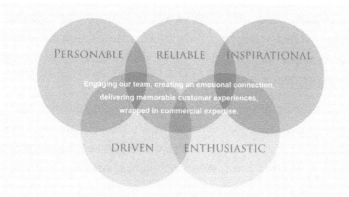

PERSONABLE   RELIABLE   INSPIRATIONAL

Engaging our team, creating an emotional connection, delivering memorable customer experiences, wrapped in commercial expertise.

DRIVEN   ENTHUSIASTIC

Discovering their values

When Brian McCarthy, Managing Director – Europe, joined Valor Hospitality five years ago, it was an organization that was underperforming and lacked energy, and had a workforce that was disillusioned and disengaged. He quickly realized that if they were going to turn the business around, they needed to create a vision for what they wanted to achieve, and recruit a team to help deliver on this.

When Brian McCarthy was appointed as Managing Director of the newly formed company, Valor Hospitality Europe, it was a business that was underperforming, had experienced several aborted sales processes, lacked investment and positioning and had a team that was downtrodden. No one's fault, merely the product of the situation, and a function of the economy at the time. He quickly realized that if they were going to turn the business around, they needed to create a vision for what they wanted to achieve, and recruit like-minded, highly skilled professionals to form a team to help deliver on this.

So, in addition to creating the business strategy and plan, they set off to create a set of values, something to define the behaviors to move them in the right direction. This was done in a completely non-democratic way, developing them from the top, but as McCarthy explained, it was done this way based on the need for speed and the lack of people. Articulating the strategy for all component parts was essential for the attraction of top talent.

The impact of these values and this new way of working have been tremendous. They've had strong financial performance, have won a series of awards around their culture and the development of their people, and employee engagement has increased from 71% to 89%.

"Aligning and measuring the performance of our team against our values has supported us to develop the culture we aspired to have, demonstrated our commitment to being an employer with a true people focus, engaged environment and attracted like-minded individuals," says McCarthy.

Bringing their values out to play

Onboarding

Once an employee is recruited and hired based on the Valor values, a key part of embedding them is the onboarding process. It includes a series of presentations about what the values are, exercises to help employees get a deeper understanding by discussing what the values mean to the business and to them personally, and a video to bring it to life through real-life stories told by employees of how they live the values.

The embedding continues throughout the onboarding through what they call "induction touchpoints". These happen after one, four, eight and twelve weeks, and focus on discussions with their manager about how they are demonstrating the values. By doing this, they ensure that the values become a natural part of discussions and behaviors, with employees committing to live them from the start of their journey and employee experience with the company.

Performance management

Another area where values are deeply embedded is with Valor's performance management process. Through the use of their online performance and succession management system, they keep track of and measure how employees are doing against both their goals and their values, with each equally weighted in the final performance assessment and rating.

The system supports discussions happening in a variety of ways about goals, behaviors and development. They include informal temperature checks and coffee chats, which can happen with anyone in the company, or more formal performance and development discussions with their manager. Together, they ensure that performance and development, both from a business and behavioral perspective, are a part of ongoing conversations and are not a once-a-year activity.

VENABLES BELL + PARTNERS

The company

Venables Bell + Partners is a San Francisco-based, independent advertising agency working with some of the most innovative and spirited brands in the world including Audi, Chipotle, Reebok, REI and 3M.

Their purpose/mission/vision

Venables Bell + Partners' purpose is to develop brands into high growth, culturally relevant performers, and ultimately to be a creative force for good in the world.

Their values

Venables Bell + Partners' three values are:

HONEST

FEARLESS

INDEPENDENT

Discovering their values

When Venables Bell + Partners first started out, everyone knew what they were doing, why they existed, and what made them unique. As Paul Venables, one of the Founders said, "this was because we (the founders) were part of every creative decision, guiding the team and connecting them to us and what we believed." But as they took on bigger accounts and the company grew in numbers, they soon realized that a lot of the new people didn't know the "why". "We felt it and could see it all around us," said Venables.

So, they very quickly brought together a group of employees for a two-day offsite, having a mix based on their job level as well as their tenure with the company, to get a wider range of perspectives. And speaking of perspectives, they took it that one step further by consulting and interviewing their clients to get their perspectives on why they work with them, seeing the business through their eyes. "We did this because we believe that values should be used to both attract internal talent and to sell ourselves to our clients. We didn't want 'x' and 'y' to be different," says Venables.

Bringing their values out to play

Many companies list their values in a handbook or put them on a poster. But never one to do things in the 'normal' way, at Venables Bell + Partners they designed double-sided plaques. On one side, it says what the company expects of employees when it comes to living the values, and on the other side, it shows what the company will do to help them in return. "It shows employees that we are in it together," says Venables, "that it's not just up to them to dance and impress us."

These plaques were created to be physical reminders to their employees, and at the same time, give a deeper feeling and understanding of what it is like to work at the company, who they are, and what is expected of them. On them, they share the values as well as what's underneath and supporting them through other behaviors and actions. As Venables says, "they codify who we are."

Fearless project

Another example of the unique way that Venables Bell + Partners bring their values to life is with something they call their 'Fearless Project'. Based on their value of 'fearless', once a year they have a challenge to their staff where they can create a project that defines what 'being fearless' means to them.

The way it works is that anyone with an idea makes a presentation and pitch to a review board, who then narrow it down to four finalists. These finalists then make their pitch to the entire company, with each employee getting a vote in the process. The winner receives $15,000 to put towards being fearless along with time off to execute their idea.

Over the years, there have been some amazing pitches and extraordinary winners. An example is an employee who wanted to raise awareness of the challenges of LGBQT+ people in countries where others are aggressive and violent towards them. With the agency's support, he created a full-length documentary to share the story and the challenges faced by this population. Another example is of an employee who again wanted to raise awareness, but this time for individuals affected by drug addiction. He developed a compelling video that captured the simulation of 12 brutal symptoms associated with opioid withdrawal, all in an effort to foster great understanding and empathy around the disease of addiction, and better support those on their paths to healing.

When asked why they put this program in place, Venables said, "We want our employees to not just work by our values, but to live them. We want to support them being fearless both in the office and outside as well."

VIRGIN ATLANTIC

The company

Founded in the mid-80s, Virgin Atlantic's purpose is 'to embrace the human spirit and let it fly' whilst Virgin Holidays was built on a belief that 'everyone can take on the world'. For its people, it recognises that an inspirational and innovative people experience connects us and helps people to be at their best.

Their purpose/mission/vision

Virgin Atlantic's mission is to be the most loved travel company.

Their values

Virgin Atlantic's three values are:

Discovering their values

In January 2019, Virgin Atlantic set off on a journey fueled by their new three-year strategy, which they call "Velocity". In order to achieve and support this strategy, they aligned, under a single strategy, their two businesses, Virgin Atlantic Airlines and Virgin Holidays, under a new set of common values, launching them at the same time as the business strategy to show their strong connection and alignment.

The decision to land on three values was intentional, as the business has a real focus on simplicity, and also follows the concept of the 'power of three' as a way to make things more meaningful and effective. "The feedback from our people is that the new values feel 'very Virgin', being authentic and describing who we are. By introducing our values, it has built a sense of belonging no matter what you do or where you work," says Suzanne Roddie, Vice President, People Experience.

After developing the new values, the second part of this important and strategic project was to develop the behaviors to sit under them. They did this by combining traditional and research-oriented approaches, resulting in four behaviors for each value to help drive the new business strategy forward.

According to Roddie, the research-oriented approach was used as, "We wanted to bring a bit of evidence and science to how our behaviors were developed, learning from what others have done to get to where we want to be in the marketplace." Working with an external provider they fed their strategy, market differentials, values descriptions and their strategic ambitions into a predictive model to look at what behaviors were needed to deliver the outcomes they desired. Alongside this, they ran a more traditional process, holding focus group sessions to ask their employees similar questions about the behaviors required to help them achieve their strategy.

Once completed, the two sets of behaviors were compared and contrasted, highlighting where their blind spots were when it came to behaviors that were required to achieve their long-term strategy. "We would never have come up with some of the behaviors had we not used this approach. It told us that we needed behaviors that we weren't yet able to articulate ourselves."

The final step in the process was to narrow it down to the final four behaviors for each value. To do this, they challenged themselves, asking – will it work for our entire diverse workforce, can we recruit based on these, and manage performance against these?

Here's an example of their fab new behaviors; this one is for their value of 'think red':

- You love to go the extra mile, above and beyond what our customers expect.

- You see things from different perspectives and are always open to change.

- You are curious and determined to find better ways to do things.

- You have a positive attitude, actively seeking to learn something new every day.

The result of these new values and behaviors are ones that are right for Virgin Atlantic today, and fuel their success in the future.

WD-40 COMPANY

The company

WD-40 Company is home to several of the world's best-known brands. The most iconic brand, WD-40 Multi-Use Product®, first appeared in the San Diego market in 1958, where it was first formulated. Today, the blue and yellow can with the little red top can be found solving problems in factories, toolboxes and homes in 176 countries. The WD-40 Company tribe of 500 people are highly engaged brand ambassadors who are passionate about delivering unique, high-value and easy to use solutions while creating positive lasting memories in all their interactions.

Their purpose/mission/vision

WD-40 Company's purpose, their 'why', is to create positive lasting memories in everything we do. We solve problems. We make things work smoothly. We create opportunities. Their "how" is to create positive lasting memories by cultivating a tribal culture of learning and teaching, which produces a highly engaged workforce who live our company's values every day.

Their values

WD-40 Company's six values are:

WE VALUE DOING THE RIGHT THING. | WE VALUE CREATING POSITIVE LASTING MEMORIES IN ALL OUR RELATIONSHIPS. | WE VALUE MAKING IT BETTER THAN IT IS TODAY. | WE VALUE SUCCEEDING AS A TRIBE WHILE EXCELLING AS INDIVIDUALS. | WE VALUE OWNING IT AND PASSIONATELY ACTING ON IT. | WE VALUE SUSTAINING THE WD-40 COMPANY ECONOMY.

Discovering their values

When WD-40 Company developed their values, they made the decision to create a hierarchy, rank-ordering them based on how they should be lived and how they should be prioritized. By doing this, employees aren't able to cherry-pick which value to use in any given situation. The hierarchical structure provides clarity to guide their decision-making and protect the best interest of the company, the culture, the brands and shareholders.

"We recognize that life is full of conflicts when it comes to living values. Sometimes you can't honor two values at the same time. That's why our values are force-ranked, and our first value, *doing the right thing*, is more important than all others," says Garry Ridge, CEO.

Another interesting decision the leadership team made when creating the values had to do with their last value, *sustaining the WD-40 Company economy*. This value relates to the company's financial wellbeing, which is something that many companies normally wouldn't include as part of their values set. The thinking was that if the tribe live all the previous five values, the financial rewards will be the applause for a job well done.

"Ranking our financial value last among our other values tells people it's important – it's one of our core values – but we will do nothing to make money that compromises any of the other values. Stating the value as sustaining the WD-40 Company economy is broader than valuing profits. When people see the word 'profit' they think, "All they care about is making money." When we talk about a thriving economy, it implies the wellbeing of all involved, not just top management." Ridge writes about this in his book titled "Helping People Win at Work.

Bringing their values out to play

At WD-40 Company, their values are truly the heart and soul of the company. They live, breathe and play by their values – every day. Their values play a crucial role in guiding the smallest to the largest decisions.

Hiring

At WD-40 Company, the first gate that any prospective tribe member needs to get past in the application process is related to their values. People exploring career opportunities with the company are encouraged not to apply if their personal values are not aligned with the Company's values. On the company's career website, they have the following message: "Please consider employment with WD-40 Company only if you feel as strongly about our values as we do." Further down the page, to the right of a big red Apply Now call to action, is the slam dunk question: "Do our company's values resonate with you?"

Prior to being able to submit an employment application, prospective employees are asked which value most closely aligns with their own and why. Applicants who do not respond to the question do not move forward in the hiring process – it's that simple. One of the first questions the talent acquisition team ask during a telephone interview is, "Please tell me about a time when you lived one of our values at work".

The company's Global Talent Director, Rachelle Snook, describes the importance of evaluating values alignment early and often in the hiring process, "The WD-40 Company tribal culture isn't for everyone. If our leaders are not rigorous in evaluating candidates' fit, which includes alignment with our values and our "why", we jeopardize the continuity of our tribal culture and ability to be self-sustaining when we invite someone to join our tribe who does not believe in what we believe".

Performance management

At WD-40 Company, their values have a large role to play in the performance review. In fact, one-quarter of the self-reported performance review is based on how they live the company's values, in addition to how well they achieve their essential functions, goals and developmental plans. During the performance review, each tribe member includes examples of when they lived each value and evaluates their ability to demonstrate the values with a 'D' grade. If they have merely "visited" the value rather than living it, they earn an 'N' grade for not consistently demonstrating the value. And, to ensure that values assessment and conversations happen frequently, managers sit down with employees every 90 days to discuss, pause, review progress, and look for any learning moments.

Another way the tribe weave their values into performance management is in the "Don't Mark My Paper, Help Me Get An A" philosophy that Ridge writes about in his book "Helping People Win at Work". An example is seen through their value of *owning it and passionately acting on it*, where instead of having leaders/coaches own the tribe member's performance review process, the tribe member is accountable for completing their quarterly performance review and for bringing to the discussion areas where they believe their developmental opportunities to be.

It's the employee who is accountable for writing their quarterly and annual reviews, owning the process, their achievements and development plan. The role of the manager/coach is to support the tribe member in their development and goal attainment. "Living our values and producing great work products are equally important. If a tribe member earns an 'A' for their performance of essential functions and does not live all the values in words and action, they may likely receive an overall 'B' grade and a performance development plan," says Snook.

ZAPPOS

The company

Zappos is an online fashion retailer that focuses on providing the best customer experience by WOWing through service. While our e-commerce platform allows our customers to purchase items like shoes, apparel, handbags, and more, we pride ourselves in also building long-lasting, mutually beneficial relationships with not only our customers, but with each other as well.

Their purpose/mission/vision

Zappos's purpose is to live and deliver WOW.

Their values

Zappos's 10 values are:

Building their values

"In 2004 we realized that we had something really special, something unique about our company and about our people, and we wanted to put a name to it," said Maritza Lewis, Employee Engagement Manager. So, in January 2005, the founders reached out to their entire workforce to ask for their thoughts, asking them to help define what would become their core values.

Hundreds of ideas were submitted, which were then dwindled down to 37 foundational themes, and then ultimately ten were selected by their workforce. It was very much an iterative and collaborative process, going back and forth and testing values with their employees over and over again. "If your employees are expected to live them, they need to be a part of developing them," says Lewis.

Zappos's ten core values were launched on February 14, 2006 (Valentine's Day ❤), and since then, have been used to guide everything they do, including how they interact with their employees, customers, community, vendors and business partners. And while the meanings behind these values have evolved as the company has changed over the years, these core values have and will remain the same.

Bringing their values out to play

At Zappos, their ten core values are more than just words, they're a way of life. They know that companies with a strong culture and a higher purpose perform better in the long run. As they continue to grow, they strive to ensure that their culture remains alive and well through a commitment to their values, as employees and as a business.

Onboarding

Every Zapponian (what Zappos call their employees), regardless of their job level or area, is required to go through their new hire training program (NHT). NHT is a four-week immersion into their culture and values, a focus on what sets Zappos apart from other companies, and how to deliver

WOW Through Service (their first core value). Throughout NHT, there is a wide variety of team-building activities, meet-and-greets from various departments, taking phone calls from real customers, and of course, lots of time spent on bringing their values to life.

One example of an exercise used to bring their values to life is the egg drop challenge. Teams are given an egg and a variety of material and then given an hour to come up with a plan before going to the second floor of the building to attempt the challenge. This exercise highlights three of their values – creating fun and a little weirdness, building open and honest relationships with communication, and building a positive team and family spirit, and is certainly more fun than hearing about them in a PowerPoint presentation.

Another requirement of NHT is that all new Zapponians are tested and evaluated to ensure they are not only a good fit for the company, but that Zappos is a good fit for them. One such test is a values presentation, which is a five to fifteen-minute presentation they must make in front of the entire company. They're asked to select one value that really resonates with them, and present on what it means to them and what they've noticed around the company in their short time as to how it's being lived. They are rated at the end by the audience, but as Lewis says, "Zapponians are pretty easy and generous in their ratings. I don't think I've ever seen anyone bomb, and if they do start to struggle, we cheer them on."

The great thing about this approach is that it is a win-win. To new Zapponians, it's a way to really stop, think and explain the values from the start, and for existing Zapponians, it helps them see the values once again through a fresh set of eyes.

Performance management

A key part of Zappos's performance management is something they call their annual "z60", or what most companies call 360 feedback. The feedback can be requested from anyone in the company, any fellow Zapponian, and is made up of around 40 behaviors that relate back to how employees are living and breathing one or more of their core values. Here are some examples of the behaviors included in the z60:

- WOW's everyone everywhere . . .
- Challenges the status quo or common wisdom . . .
- Things EVEN BIGGER . . .
- Gets sh!t done with less . . .
- Never believes the statement, "It can't be done" . . .

For each question, assessors have to say how often their colleague displays the behavior – never, not really, sometimes, usually or always. Interestingly, they can only answer 'always' up to five times for a set of questions. "This is done because we want each employee to have areas to improve. We know that as a business we don't know everything, and that we will only succeed if our business and our people continue to learn and continue to grow," says Lewis.

Zappos has three other interesting twists to the process. The first is that results are not shared with managers, but just with the individual who has been evaluated by their peers. The other is that employees are also asked to evaluate themselves in the process, comparing how they think they live and breathe the core values against what our fellow Zapponians think. And finally, they are asked to call out certain Zapponians that they believe are inspiring, who they go to for advice, who has the most potential, etc. "The z60 challenges us to reach out to those employees we admire and have a cup of coffee or a quick lunch so that we can connect and ultimately learn and grow from the people who were mentioned in the survey. To be honest, it's a wonderful and challenging new twist on how to improve and evolve on a personal and professional level," says Lewis.

CHAPTER 7

Additional pandemic plays

Introduction

There are moments in time that need to be documented, where you need to capture the thoughts, experiences, and actions that really mattered, and that made a significant difference and a lasting impact. And the COVID-19 pandemic has certainly been one of those moments, throwing the world and businesses into a state of chaos and confusion, leaving everyone to sort out solutions in a time jam-packed with unknowns, and with more questions than answers.

But in the face of these challenges and uncertainty, companies around the world have risen up and have not only brought their values out to play, but have used them time and time again in new, innovative, and impactful ways. Regardless of country, industry, or demographics, we have seen what I call "**Values Warriors**" emerge, armed with their values, and ready to be a part of the solution as they protect, support, and care for their communities and for their people.

> "Warriors aren't born, and they are not made. They create themselves through trial and error and by their ability to conquer their own frailties and faults."
>
> **Philip J. Messina**

And that is why I've added this new chapter to this book. For although it was just published in December 2019, just a few months before the pandemic began, I thought it was critical to capture the moment and capture the actions. And so this new chapter contains 24 wonderful new plays from "Values Warriors" from companies around the world who have truly lived their values during the pandemic.

When reading the plays, please keep these things in mind:

- **There's so much more** - each company did so much more than what's included in their play. But as with previous plays appearing in this book, I've spread out the topics and actions between companies so that you get a mix of different ways and approaches.

- **The pandemic isn't/wasn't over** - at the time these plays were written, the pandemic was still very much going on. However, since this book will hopefully be around (and read) far after the pandemic has finished, it was written in the past tense.

- **These stories happened at different times** - the stories told in the plays took place at different times throughout the pandemic. For example, some took place at the lockdown phase, when except for essential workers, all others needed to work from home or be put on furlough, where depending on the government they could receive all or a portion of their salary. Others took place when offices and operations were opening up, and companies were dealing with bringing their employees back into the workplace.

AND-E

The company

Aioi Nissay Dowa Insurance Europe (AND-E) is the European arm of one of the world's largest insurers, providing motor insurance to Toyota and Lexus customers across Europe. They're also the parent company of the largest telematics (black-box) insurance brand in the UK, Insure the Box. Their vision is "To lead the way in connected mobility protection."

Their values

AND-E's six values, or what they call behaviors, are:

1. Achieving	2. Collaborating	3. Engaging
4. Innovating	5. Leading	6. Learning

Bringing their values out to play

For their people

AND-E used their values in a variety of ways that added up to support employees, families, and ultimately their customers throughout the pandemic, such as:

- **Setting employees up for success** - it started by setting their employees up for success as they transitioned from offices and call centers to working from home. This was done by creating detailed manager and employee guides within 48 hours of lockdown to help employees understand how to work in the new world and in the new ways, ranging from tips on how to set up workspaces to how to stay happy and healthy working from home.

And not to leave out the children, they also created "homeschooling kits" that were sent to parents containing supplies such as adhesive white board paper, pens, and craft supplies to help them with their new teaching responsibilities and to keep their children engaged at home.

- **Financial support** - it continued by providing financial support to their employees, living their value of "**innovating**" to create a flexible approach to work so that employees would receive full pay throughout lockdown regardless of their personal circumstances. They did this by creating "gateways" that employees could pass through to allow them the time to balance work and personal commitments. The gateways included three options: to work different work patterns, to take holiday entitlement, or to take emergency leave, which they increased from 2 to ten days.

This approach worked for all but a few employees, but as Andy Preacher, People and Culture Director UK said, "If they ran out of options and we saw that they were trying their best to support the business, we still paid them their full salary."

- **Connected communities** - they also created "connected communities," something that aligns with their vision as well as their value of "**collaborating.**" They did this by setting up a variety of virtual spaces that were run by volunteers and covered a broad range of subjects for colleagues and families to maintain and create new contacts, learn something new or simply have fun. "We wanted to include the whole colleague, not just the at work colleague, so we invited all family members," said Preacher.

These activities ranged from beginner chess or java programming classes, to sushi making classes to reflect their Japanese ownership, to mindfulness sessions, to family quiz night. They even ran a creative kids corner that included activities such as creating a new company logo or designing a car of the future.

"This has been great for increasing connections between colleagues as they spoke to people they had never spoken to before and built new relationships," said Preacher.

- **Welcome back to the office packs** - the final example involves packs that AND-E created as a way to thank and welcome employees back to the office at the end of lockdown. They included a welcome message from their CEO thanking everyone for the flexibility and commitment they had given to the company, hand sanitizer, washable face masks, and, because they were sent on International Chocolate Day, a bar of chocolate.

We put in place all of the safety precautions so that colleagues would be safe in the office, but we wanted to do more. The packs were a nod to say that we get what you're going through coming back into the office, that we're thinking of you, and that we're here to help you feel safe" said Preacher.

ATOS

The company

Atos, a global leader in digital transformation, has a history that spans a century. From Fredrik Rosing Bull first creating the tabulating machine, the predecessor to the supercomputer, to today being Europe's number one digital services provider. Every day their 110,000 people in 73 countries are developing and implementing innovative digital solutions that support the business transformation of clients and address the environmental and social challenges we all face.

Their values

Atos's seven values are:

1. Accountability	2. Trust	3. Service
4. Innovation	5. Excellence	6. Social Well Being
7. Operational Competitiveness		

Bringing their values out to play

For the community

At Atos, their values were seen time and time again in how they helped the global fight against COVID-19. Here are a few ways they did this:

- **Helped local authorities contain the spread of the virus** - they designed EpiSYS, an Epidemic Management System (EMS) that gave healthcare professionals a precise overview of an epidemiological situation by storing and managing all patient data and data related to the virus, including tracking and tracing patient incident reports, in real-time.

- **Mobilized supercomputers and machine learning to speed up research** - around the world, Atos' high-performance computers, which count thousands of times faster than standard computers, were used by research teams involved in the fight against COVID-19.

- **Shared data science skills with the research community** - they took part in the "COVID–19 Dataset Challenge," an international competition launched by the White House, asking AI researchers to apply machine learning tools and techniques to help provide answers to key questions about the disease. Atos dedicated a team of ten experts to work on the project.

For their people

Atos also lived their values in their approach to supporting their people. Aligning with "We are Atos" that focuses on the full life cycle of their employee experience through five key areas – Diversity & Inclusion, Social Value, Wellbeing, Life@Work, and Customer Experience, they made sure to have something for everyone.

Here are a few of the many examples:

- **Manager helpline** - as more and more questions were coming in from managers, they decided to set up a manager helpline. "We wanted to take some of the pain away from our managers, letting them know that we were there for them," said Cheryl Allen, HR Director. "It's also improved the overall credibility of HR, with managers seeing our value, which will improve our relationships going forward."

- **"How to have a holiday at home" webinar** - they ran a variety of events for their workforce, including webinars and videos on how to make the most of a holiday at home, something many were doing during lockdown. Ideas were presented from different perspectives so that colleagues could relate and learn from them. A dedicated virtual event webinar brought ideas together: they ranged from a parent sharing how to have a camping holiday in your backyard, to a graduate living at home with his parents who talked about a cooking holiday of meals from around the world, to an employee living on their own who did everything virtually, from riding roller coasters to going on safari tours.

- **Kids summer camp** - with school over and holiday clubs reduced, Atos decided to run a two-week virtual summer camp open to all employee's children to support working parents and carers. It was run as a community, with parents having to conduct a one hour session based on any talent or skill they selected. Sessions ranged from French and sign language lessons, to karate, to how to make play-dough, to a dinosaur party. They even brought in business-related topics such as how to code and information on climate change and diversity. "What was great about it, and something I didn't expect, is that so many people have reached out who don't have children to say how brilliant it is because it shows the caring side of Atos outside of the normal employment relationship," said Allen.

BANCO SANTANDER

The company

Banco Santander (Santander) is a Spanish multinational commercial bank and financial services company that was founded in 1857 when Queen Isabella II of Spain signed a Royal Decree authorizing the incorporation of Banco Santander. Initially intended to facilitate trade between the Port of Santander, in northern Spain, and Latin America, it now operates in ten main markets, servicing over 145 million customers.

Their values

Santander's three values are:

1. Simple	2. Personal	3. Fair

Bringing their values out to play

For the community

Santander was committed to their customers and the wider community throughout the pandemic, showing it in a variety of ways. A great example involves a story about a customer in a remote area of Scotland. The customer came in with bags of coins that he wanted put into his bank account. The employee could have turned him away, but instead the team treated him with empathy, agreeing to help. As it turns out, the customer explained that his only local shop was closed due to the pandemic and so his only option to get food and drinks was via online shopping. Had the employee not helped, he would not have been able to shop throughout the pandemic. "This is how you live your mission and values, serving your customers as individuals, as people," said Daniel Strode, Group Director of Culture & Strategy.

Here are a few other examples:

- **Virtual volunteering** - the pandemic did not stop the volunteering efforts of Santander employees, as they continued to devote their time in the move from face-to-face to virtual. These efforts included the regular programs on financial training, legal advice, and mentoring for women who have been victims of gender-based violence, as well as launching several new social initiatives covering new needs such as making face masks for healthcare workers and customers, and a telephone "befriending" service for the elderly living alone or in care homes or hospitals.

- **"Together Solidarity" Fund** - in order to support the global effort to combat coronavirus, Santander created a fund that contributed to initiatives to combat COVID-19. The fund of €100 million was financed initially by executives donating a portion of their salaries, with additional contributions coming from voluntary employee donations, third parties, and the Group subsidiaries. Contributions were used throughout Santander's home markets to buy medical equipment and support research into the virus through collaboration with universities and other bodies, as well as protecting vulnerable groups most affected by the disease in several countries.

For their people

Santander also made it a priority to protect the health of their 200,000 employees worldwide. Whether it was putting in place the technology and tools to enable more than 100,000 employees to work remotely, or establishing special opening hours, selective closures, shifts, and additional protective measures to protect the health of employees who dealt directly with their customers, they balanced the needs of their workforce and their customers.

One way they did this was to give employees the freedom to work in a way that met their individual circumstances, bringing to life their value of "***personal,***" which talks about personalizing the needs of each and every employee (and customer) to feel valued and treated as an individual. They did this with branch employees, creating three categories:

1. Those that could work their full hours at the branch serving customers.

2. Those that could work the majority of their hours but couldn't go into the branch due to health or personal commitments.

3. Those that could only work a few hours and could not come into the branch.

"We redeployed our employees to work their hours in ways where it would matter most, whether it was answering emails, learning new skills, or checking in with colleagues to make sure they were OK. We asked ourselves, 'if you could only work two hours, what would it be?'" said Strode. And, regardless of hours worked, all employees received full pay from the company.

Another way was with wellbeing, where they not only changed their branding to "be healthy at home," but they moved to a more holistic approach, expanding the focus in areas such as mental wellbeing. Through a variety of policies and procedures that supported and encouraged wellbeing, in addition to apps and other tools to make wellbeing content more readily available, they gave employees permission and the opportunity to take care of their own personal wellbeing.

BREWDOG

The company

BrewDog is an independent Scottish brewery and pub chain founded in 2007 by two men and a dog who were on a mission to make other people as passionate about great craft beer as they were. They now employ over 1,000 employees in 24 countries, run 101 pubs, and manufacture over 200 different craft beers.

Their values

BrewDog's five values are called their "charter," because, as Fiona Hunter, Head of Employee Engagement says, "They feel like a collective commitment to act because they were created in such a collaborative way."

1. **Our mission is to make other people as passionate about great craft beer as we are.**
   World class craft beer is our true north.

2. **We make things that we love. From scratch.**
   If we don't love it. We don't do it. Ever

3. **We are community owned and fiercely independent.**
   In an industry dominated by multinational conglomerates, we are making a stand for independence, a stand for authenticity, and a stand for craft.

4. **We are committed to being a great employer.**
   Our long-term destiny will be completely dependent on how well we look after our amazing people.

5. **We want to show that business can be a force for good.**
   We believe in radical transparency, in looking after the environment, in doing things differently and we believe in giving back.

Bringing their values out to play

One of BrewDog's values is that they "**want to show that business can be a force for good,**" doing so by looking for opportunities to do things differently and by giving back. They've lived this across the business in many ways throughout COVID-19, but here are a sampling of them:

For the community:

- In the UK, they made and donated over £1 million worth of BrewDog sanitizer to health care charities, key frontline workers and National Health Care (NHS) hospitals.

- In the U.S., they made and donated BrewDog sanitizer to health care charities as well as police officers and firefighters.

- They made and sold thousands of their BrewDog NHS Heroes packs, with the profits from every single case donated to the Help NHS Heroes charity.

- To help their Columbus, Ohio community, they supplied their water at cost price to retailers who needed it, and also donated water to Gladden Community House Food Pantry and the YMCA Homeless Shelter.

- They volunteered their trucks and drivers to do home delivery of meals to those in isolation in their local communities.

- They shared the recipes for every single beer they've ever made for free on their website so that people could brew beer at their homes.

For their people:

- To help protect as many jobs as possible, many of their senior team volunteered to take pay cuts, and the two co-founders are forgoing all of their salary for 2020.

- They improved their Employee Assistance Plan (EAP) so that employees would have the right level of support and tools throughout the pandemic.

- They introduced programs such as their virtual "online bar," giving employees the opportunity to share their passions and provide support to one another.

- They sent a case of beer to each of their team members on furlough.

And as if all of this wasn't enough, the company has said that "When all of this is over, we are going to buy everyone a beer."

DELIVERY HERO

The company

Delivery Hero is the world's leading local delivery platform, and is on a mission to deliver amazing experiences – fast, easy and to your door. With their global headquarters in Berlin, Germany, they operate in over 40 markets with more than 25,000 employees.

Their values

Delivery Hero's three values are:

1. We always aim higher	2. We deliver solutions	3. We are Heroes because we care

Bringing their values out to play

For the community

Driven by their value "**we are Heroes because we care,**" Delivery Hero broadened their social responsibility to support local communities in their battle against the spread of COVID-19. By partnering with local governments, public institutions, and charity organisations, their brands across more than 40 countries played a key role in ensuring people receive the support and goods they need, including:

- **Helping high risk groups** - aware of the challenges older generations faced due to the pandemic, their Turkish brand Yemeksepeti collaborated with the governing body of Istanbul to provide a hotline for residents aged over 65. Residents could call to order groceries without extra service charges or delivery fees.

- **Providing essential goods and services** - to support the government's quarantine efforts while fulfilling a basic need for groceries, meal kits, and cooked meals, their Middle East brand Talabat joined forces with the Kuwaiti government, providing grocery delivery services from their Co-Op supermarkets free of charge.

- **Delivering medicine** - with many communities facing limitations to leave their homes, Delivery Hero brands supported governments in delivering medical supplies. Their Panama brand Appetito24 partnered with the local government to deliver medicine to more than 30,000 people aged over 65.

- **Meal donations** - Delivery Hero's teams around the world went above and beyond to provide meals where they were most needed. As of August 2020, they had already donated more than 300,000 meals to frontline workers and communities in need.

"Caring for each other and our ecosystem is a core part of our values at Delivery Hero. We have a duty to help and provide solutions for people trying to cope with this health crisis. The best way we can support is by providing as many people as possible with the supplies needed to stay at home. By using our existing infrastructure and collaborating with partners on the ground, we can ensure that our local communities get the supplies and care they need," said Niklas Östberg, CEO & Co-Founder.

For their people

Delivery Hero's value "**we are Heroes because we care**" was also woven into how they supported their people throughout the pandemic. An example is their focus and commitment to the wellbeing of their workforce, which was shown through:

- **Global Employee Assistance Plan (EAP)** - although an EAP is not a common benefit in many of their 43 countries, Delivery Hero felt it was important to put in place an EAP hotline in each and every one. Pushing it out globally in only four weeks, it provided the necessary free and confidential advice and support to their workforce to cope with the complex combination of personal and work-related issues.

- **Wellbeing events** - they ran a variety of wellbeing events to focus on both community and connection. This included virtual Friday night DJ sessions and live concerts where they pooled the collective and often unknown talents of their workforce. As Jeri Doris, Chief People Officer said, "It was amazing seeing people from all parts of the company come together online. From DJ sets to flute concerts, there was a real sense of shared experience and community."

These initiatives, as well as everything else they did to show their employees they cared, were grounded and based on feedback from their employees. "My mantra throughout was to never make assumptions. I was surprised at how open and honest the feedback and comments were, but it really helped us to tailor our communications and also know that we needed to double down on mental health support," said Doris.

EPIDEMIC SOUND

The company

Epidemic Sound is a music company that licenses its tracks to content creators all over the world. Founded in 2009 by award-winning Swedish music, TV, and Internet entrepreneurs, Epidemic Sound doesn't represent music, it owns it, buying directly from composers when tracks are created to give today's generation of musicians a new way to make a living making music.

Their values

Epidemic Sound's five values are:

1.	Let's celebrate	2.	Be a force for good
3.	Rebel without a pause	4.	Do the hustle
5.	Come together		

Bringing their values out to play

For the community

During the pandemic, Epidemic Sound missioned themselves through their value of "*come together*" to activate and engage their creator community through various challenges in a campaign called "Come2gether." Some challenges they included were:

- **"Work from Home" movie trailer challenge** - with half the world being stuck in quarantine, the need for fun and engaging content had never been more present. So Epidemic Sound created this challenge

to make the "dopest trailer for a movie about your experience working from home" as they announced on their website. They received
260 entries, with three winners receiving $500 and a yearly Epidemic
subscription. Competition was fierce, but they were able to settle on
three clear winners who led the way with their creativity and positive
outlook.

- **"Pass the beat" challenge** - they asked their music creators to
collaborate on a track, to keep the creativity flowing during the lockdown, and to one by one "pass the beat" around. The challenge
included 20 music creators that had 24 hours to work on the track
individually before passing it on for the next person to add layers.
The collaborators were located across nine major locations, including
Stockholm, Texas, Los Angeles, and Portland, that had similar locked-
down circumstances. The result is this wonderful mix: https://www.
epidemicsound.com/blog/passthebeat/

For their people

The value of "*come together*," which talks about uniting, collaborating,
and doing things together, was also shown by how Epidemic Sound
treated their people during the pandemic. "Our employees are wired
for connection, with this being why many join and stay with the company,"
said Maria Waddington, Chief People & Culture Officer. But as the company closed their offices, they needed to find new ways to do this, moving
to a more digital approach much in the same way as their business and
products.

Digital soon found a home in weekly live updates that provided business
updates and a Q&A with their CEO, all transparently sharing both progress and thinkings. Social activities were also moved to a digital format,
enhancing the digital togetherness. One example was their social distanc-
ing discos, where they leveraged the musical talents of their workforce
to run discos for their entire workforce and their families. And speaking
of family, they moved their office choir to a digital choir, allowing family
members to join in on the digital experience and the fun. These both gave
employees opportunities to come together and also to celebrate, which

is another Epidemic Sound value.

But as with most companies, not everything was discos and singing throughout the pandemic, and they had the difficult challenge of making 79 of their employees redundant due to business changes. But living their values yet again, they did this in a respectful and people-focused approach, setting up a "One Epidemic Network" to support, coach and provide opportunities for these important members of their team. "It was part of our core to do it in an empathetic way with a big heart. It's what our employees expected of us, both those that were leaving and those that were staying, and if we had done it differently they would have been disappointed in us," said Waddington.

EVE SLEEP

The company

In 2015, eve Sleep's founders had an idea to change how you shop for mattresses, letting you order one at a click of a button and deliver it in a box along with a 100-nights at-home trial. Five years on and eve are now a Sleep Wellness brand and provide a whole range of sleep-inducing goodies to solve those horrible little worries we all have as we nod off to sleep, all still delivered straight to your door. With their 55 employees, they're on a mission to unleash the power of sleep wellness for all.

Their values

eve Sleep's five values are:

1. We are experts in support	2. We keep things simple
3. We are yellow	4. We don't believe in being sheep
5. We won't sleep until you do	

Bringing their values out to play

eve Sleep's values were launched in February 2020, one month before they went into lockdown. Many companies in this situation would have waited until things were back to "normal" before embedding and integrating them, but instead, the business decided to use this opportunity to weave their values into a variety of initiatives. This showed their employees the values were here to stay and were critical now and in the future to how they ran their business, treated their people, and supported one another.

For the community:

One of eve Sleep's values is that "**we are experts in support,**" which talks about flying the flag of wellbeing, and being uncompromising in making the lives of their customers, and each other, better. Here are a few ways they helped and supported not just their customers, but the community, at the start of the pandemic:

- **Donations to hospitals** - to play a role in improving sleep quality and wellbeing for as many people as possible during this critical time, eve Sleep donated mattresses and pillows to a number of hospitals to help their staff get much-needed rest between shifts.

- **Donations to key workers** - to support key workers, employees were given the opportunity to nominate key workers in their life and send them a sleep well gift box including pillows and bedding to help them with their own well being, support them through this time and put a smile on their faces. These boxes were given to traditional key workers who supported employees throughout the pandemic in meaningful ways, even having one employee gift a box to their local butcher!

For their people:

The new values also created opportunities to shine through in eve Sleep's people initiatives, including the introduction of these three programs:

- **Simply the Best program** - the Simply the Best recognition program was launched in week two of lockdown, and aligns with their value "**we are yellow,**" which talks about celebrating successes and efforts. The program has been great for driving awareness of the new values, making employees feel appreciated, and helping employees learn more about the business and each other during these challenging times.

- **Small Acts of Kindness program** - another new program has been the Small Acts of Kindness program, aligning to the value "**we are experts in support.**" Small tokens were sent out to employees to support them with their struggles, with gifts ranging from flowers to plants, and even dry hair shampoo for one employee who was without water for an entire week.

- **Make Someone Smile program** - the final example is the Make Someone Smile program, which aligns to their value *"we are yellow,"* focusing on the part of the value that talks about positivity and waking up on the right side of the bed. Everyone was given the name of a colleague and told they could spend £5 to send them a secret gift. This not only brought a smile to everyone's face, but also helped them stay connected and supported, sending the message that they're all in it together.

FLIPKART

The company

Flipkart is an Indian e-commerce company that was started in 2007 by selling books online. Now, over a decade later, they are India's largest online marketplace and one of India's leading technology powerhouses that is disrupting the way India shops online.

Their values

Flipkart's four values, which they call their "ABCs with integrity," are:

1. Audacity	2. Bias for Action
3. Customer First	4. Integrity

Bringing their values out to play

To the community

When the pandemic hit in India, Flipkart quickly stepped up to ensure essential items could be delivered across the country, adapting and changing existing systems and practices to meet these new and demanding needs. Being "**customer first,**" one of their core values, they brought in their other values of "**audacity**" and "**bias for action**" to come up with ways to connect the entire ecosystem to achieve the end-to-end delivery that was necessary for their customers.

"Innovation sprang up during these challenging times, with the team coming together across multiple functions to build solutions in quick time to service our customer, translating ideas into action with a sense of urgency and a sense of pride," said Krishna Raghavan, Chief People Officer.

Here are a few ways they did this:

- **Local taxi drivers** - with a large number of local taxi drivers not working due to reduced travel, Flipkart brought them in to deliver essential items to customers, supplementing their normal delivery network to meet the increasing demands.

- **Re-tooled fulfillment centers** - fulfillment centers were modified to be able to focus on and deliver essential items in a much larger geographical area.

- **Local merchants in Kiranas** - they partnered with small and large local merchants to connect and deliver merchandise to customers in need.

For their people

The story of how Flipkart supported their employees throughout the pandemic is also firmly grounded around their values, and also around safety. Time and time again they went above and beyond to support their 120,000 employees, the majority of which were working in fulfillment centers across India, whether they were permanent or contract workers.

"We thought about the entire lifecycle, from awareness to prevention and finally, in how to deal with the virus. We asked ourselves - how can the company step in and support our employees at the various stages in the best way?" said Raghavan.

Here are a few ways the company supported their employees:

- **Awareness sessions** - they conducted over 4,000 awareness sessions with their employees across the country, emphasizing the importance of safety and how to minimize their exposure through certain precautionary measures.

- **On-site doctors** - Flipkart did something that was an industry-first by deploying doctors to be located on site at a number of their fulfillment centers, being there to take care of their employees at any point in time.

- **Testing** - with private testing in India not being comprehensive and mature, they entered into relationships with diagnostic labs across the country to make tests easily available to their entire workforce.

- **Extended life insurance** - they extended life insurance cover for their contract workers, increasing their entitlement through intermediaries to be the same level as provided to their permanent workers.

- **Coronavirus fund** - they created a fund that would be paid to employees should they get the coronavirus to cover any ad hoc expenses.

Flipkart employees also stepped up to focus on safety by coming up with simple yet effective inventions to maintain high standards of hygiene, living their values of "**audacity**" and "**bias for action.**" An example was a foot-powered touchless hand sanitizing dispenser that was developed by employees at one of its fulfilment centers, and was then replicated at its fulfilment centers across the country.

MACMILLAN

The company

Macmillan Cancer Support is one of the largest British charities and provides physical, financial, and emotional support for those with cancer, so they can live life as fully as they can.

Their values

Macmillan's seven behaviors and five supporting experience principles that guide employees to deliver a consistent Macmillan experience are:

Behaviors:	Experience principles:
1. Delivering results	1. Empathy
2. Learning & improvement	2. Proximity
3. Communicating & influencing	3. Resolution
4. Acting as one team	4. Inspiration
5. Enabling change	5. Empowerment
6. Making decisions	
7. Engaging people	

Bring their values out to play

For their people

One of the challenges Macmillan faced at the start of the pandemic was how to support and communicate with their furloughed employees, which was 36% of their total workforce. With guidance from the government reducing the contact with employees, they needed to find a way to stay connected and provide support to this important group of employees.

So living behaviors such as "**learning & improvement,**" which is about looking for ways to improve and do things better, they created a separate communications platform for furloughed employees, mirroring their Top Banana communications portal that was used for the rest of the workforce. They took this extra step so that furloughed employees would feel connected to the business and to each other during these times of uncertainty. "The longer employees were on furlough the more they worried and wondered if they were still needed by the organization. We wanted to stop these feelings by helping them feel a part of the business, reminding them that the company was looking forward to them returning," said Sam Dewey, Reward & Wellbeing Manager.

The platform evolved over time to include biweekly newsletters and surveys to gain an understanding of how employees were feeling and what support they required. "It's been a learning curve for us, showing us the importance of creating something personal and relevant for this group of employees," said Dewey.

Another challenge was supporting the wellbeing of their workforce. Driven by behaviors such as "**embracing change,**" which involves constantly looking at the bigger picture and to better ways of doing things, the organization acted on this value in countless ways, such as:

- **Wellbeing platform** - prior to the pandemic, Macmillan had identified a need for a wellbeing platform, and were considering putting one in place. But as the pandemic started, and wellbeing became a focus and priority, they decided to move quicker on this important initiative. So after trialing a new wellbeing platform, they launched it to their entire workforce, including furloughed employees, delivering an online platform providing education, support, and tools to meet the needs of their employee's personal wellbeing.

- **Social connections** - "Working at a charity is very social, very fun, because everyone is here for the same reason and the same purpose. But with this disappearing overnight, we needed to find a way to recreate these social connections and unify the workforce," said Dewey. So with the help of an activity calendar, Dewey and the team organized daily activities such as quizzes, bingo, workouts, meditations, and cooking to name a few. It's been such a success that it's evolved into "Green Get Togethers," aligning with their "Go Green" branding, and continuing to deliver social connections in different and meaningful ways.

- **Including volunteers** - prior to the pandemic, Macmillan's Employee Assistance Plan (EAP) was only available to their 2,000 permanent employees. But seeing the need to also support their 20,000 volunteers, they made the decision to extend and provide EAP to them as well. "The pandemic really made us think of our workforce differently, making sure we met the needs of our whole team," said Dewey. Since this is not a normal practice, it really brings "**acting as one team**" to life as it shows the personal care delivered to each and every important member of their workforce.

MICROSOFT

The company

Microsoft is a multinational technology company that develops, man-ufactures, licenses, supports, and sells computer software, consumer electronics, personal computers, and related services. Their mission is to transform the way people live, play and connect through great technology, developing new ways for people to interact with technology at home, at work, and on the move, while transforming education and public services and supporting the economy.

Their values

Microsoft's three values are:

1. Respect	2. Integrity	3. Accountability

Bringing their values out to play

For the community

At Microsoft, they were committed to doing their part to protect the health and wellbeing of the communities in which they operate, provid-ing technology, tips and resources to their customers to help them do their best while working remotely. Here are just two of the many ways they did this:

- **Provided local support** - throughout their local communities, Microsoft jumped in to provide local support. An example was in the Puget Sound region, where the company was founded, and where they made the decision to continue to pay their vendor hourly service workers their regular wages even if their work hours were reduced during the pandemic. These included individuals who worked at their cafes, drove their shuttles and supported their on-site tech and audio-visual needs, doing this to recognize the hardship that lost work would mean for them.

- **Provided help for 25 million job seekers** - Microsoft identified that one of the ways to genuinely create an inclusive recovery was to provide easier access to digital tools to improve the skills of people hardest hit by job losses, including those with lower incomes, women, and underrepresented minorities. To help address this need, they launched a global skills initiative aimed at bringing more digital skills to 25 million people worldwide by the end of 2020. This initiative brought together every part of their company, combining existing and new resources from LinkedIn, GitHub, and Microsoft.

For their people

The same level of care was given to Microsoft employees, living values such as "*respect,*" respecting the new challenges their workforce was facing and respecting their individual and unique set of needs. Here are two of the many ways they did this:

- **Virtual interviews** - Microsoft's recruitment efforts did not slow down during the pandemic, which meant they needed to quickly find an alternative to face-to-face interviews. Like others, they made the decision to bring them online by moving to virtual interviews, but then took it to the next level by creating a playbook to clearly explain the process and how to be successful in a virtual environment. This is a great example of respecting the changing needs of both hiring managers and candidates, creating a solution to set them up for success, overcoming the new challenges they were facing.

- **Role-modeled maintaining balance and health** - recognizing the importance and challenges of maintaining the balance of work and home and of a healthy lifestyle during the pandemic, Microsoft decided to bring in their leaders to help role model it to their workforce. They had leaders share personal stories of the challenges they were having and what they were doing to overcome them, signaling that everyone was having challenges in one way, and that it was OK to talk about it so that together they could address and overcome them. One such post was by a leader in the U.S. who talked of the challenge of not being able to see her elderly parents due to lockdown. The reaction by employees encapsulated all of their values as many wrote to the leader to say that they would be happy to pop in and check in on her parents.

The company

The National Basketball Association (NBA) is a global sports and media business based in the U.S. that is passionate about growing and celebrating the game of basketball. In addition to running the league's on-court activities through their four leagues, they also manage media relationships, develop marketing partnerships, and oversee licensing of NBA merchandise. Off the court, they're deeply committed to social responsibility, supporting education, youth and family development, and health-related causes through NBA Cares.

Their values

The NBA's four values, or what they call the "four corners of our court," are:

1. Integrity	2. Respect
3. Teamwork	4. Innovation

Bringing their values out to play

For the community

The NBA is not just viewed as a basketball organization, but as an organization that is a social icon. The world looks at how they'll think and act when it comes to not just sports, but to political and social issues as well. Guided by their values, they've shown time and again how their values are more than just words.

This has been the case throughout the pandemic, when the league used its vast digital footprint and the powerful voices of teams, players, coaches, doctors, and others across the NBA family to launch "NBA Together" - a global community and social engagement campaign aimed at supporting, engaging, educating, and inspiring youth, families, and fans in response to the coronavirus pandemic.

The program was centered around these four pillars:

- **Know the Facts** - this pillar is about amplifying the latest global health and safety information, sharing guidelines and resources so that important and life-saving facts are known. To support this pillar, the NBA launched a "Coronavirus Information For NBA Fans" webpage, providing content and links for their global fans, plus the latest information on developments in their regions and how to best protect themselves and others from the virus.

  The NBA and WNBA also used the influential voices of players, coaches, and legends through public service announcements to inform fans on the best ways to stay safe and healthy in both their body and mind as the world faces the rapidly changing and evolving pandemic.

- **Acts of Caring** - this pillar is about shining a light on the power of community and volunteerism by inspiring one million big and small acts of kindness. The NBA called on players, fans and the general public to share ways they were supporting friends, families, and communities by posting photos and videos with the hashtag #NBATogether on Twitter, Instagram, Facebook, and TikTok.

- **Expand Your Community** - this pillar is about encouraging fans to expand their communities through content, activities, and virtual engagement in an effort to stay physically and mentally healthy and active. It included the launch of "Jr. NBA at Home," an interactive content series for young people who were unable to play with their friends and teammates, but still wanted to be active, working on their game and connected with the NBA.

  In addition, the NBA engaged with education and wellness partners such as Discovery Education, Scholastic Inc., and NBA Math Hoops, to promote existing resources for students and parents that have been adapted for at-home learning. And in an effort to combat the higher levels of anxiety and stress during these uncertain times, the NBA, in partnership with Kaiser Permanente and Headspace, provided mental wellness and resiliency resources and tools to encourage fans to be mindful of their mental wellness and the wellbeing of those around them.

- **NBA Together Live** - this pillar was about keeping people socially connected with their favorite players and teams. They did this with live daily interviews with members of the NBA family, taking questions from fans on Instagram live, and streaming classic games.

ORDERGROOVE

The company

Ordergroove is a U.S. commerce technology platform that is on a mission to simplify consumers' lives by transforming the buying experience. They make consumers' lives easier via removal of friction, and help their retail customers by moving from one-and-done transactions to recurring, commerce-enabled customer relationships.

Their values

Ordergroove's four values are:

1. What you see is what you get	2. We're in it to win it
3. We drive results	4. We're comfortable being uncomfortable

Bringing their values out to play

For their people

At Ordergroove, they worked as a team to lean into their values to lead them through unprecedented and challenging times. Along the way, the team learned valuable lessons about what worked (and what didn't!).

One example was how they redesigned their flexible work policy, using their values as a "gut check," going through them one by one as they developed an approach to use moving forward. Here's how else they leaned into individual values:

- **What you see is what you get** - this value is about feeling safe to be your authentic self, and was used throughout the pandemic as they encouraged employees to share the chaos at home as they moved to working remotely. One example was holding a contest for the most creative way to set up your office space, celebrating the authenticity of what you see is what you get. Employees shared photos ranging from using toasters, kid's easels, anything and everything showing their new human working space, including one person who put their dining room chairs on the table to create a standing desk. Another way was by constantly reminding employees to never say you are sorry for an interruption, whether that's from kids, pets, roommates, whatever, because that was your authentic life at that moment.

- **We're in it to win it** - this value is about getting to the right answer, no matter who comes up with it, focusing on collaborating to hit their goals. To support this during the pandemic, Ordergroove set up new Slack channels and additional recurring meetings to recreate the "drive-by" conversations. Employees leaned into this value as well, stepping up to cover for colleagues impacted more by the pandemic without a second thought, collaborating and winning together.

- **We drive results** - this value is about focusing on results and outcomes, and not just actions. This was seen in the decision to close their offices earlier than the government mandate, sending the message that it doesn't matter where you work, but rather the results you deliver. It also was a part of how the team celebrated the achievement of goals, creating a biweekly team toast and a "good news" channel in Slack to make sure they were recognizing the results being delivered during the challenging economic downturn.

- **We're comfortable being uncomfortable** - this value is about riding the rollercoaster, and as Karen Weeks, SVP People said, "This pandemic has been the mother of all coasters, but we were up for the challenge."

They tried and tested new approaches and programs, constantly asking themselves, "OK, what do we do now?" For instance, to combat Zoom fatigue, the team decided to focus on activities that were easy for employees to do from home, like creating cards for seniors to give back to the community, or submitting ideas that were easy for employees, such as new recipes people were trying while being home.

As Weeks said, "While there was definitely burnout and fatigue with all the change and the emotional rollercoaster we all were on, the ongoing changes didn't throw us, and everyone was able to adapt quickly."

PCH

The company

Plymouth Community Homes (PCH) are a leading, growing, independent housing association with a clear social purpose, providing homes and services people want and can afford. They are the largest social housing landlord in Plymouth, UK, responsible for over 16,000 properties providing homes to over 35,000 people, and pride themselves in doing the right things by their residents and employees.

Their values

PCH's four values are:

1. Do the right things	2. Care
3. Respect	4. Listen

Bringing their values out to play

For the community

When the country and their residents were in lockdown, PCH jumped in to provide help and support to them, living each and every value along the way. Here are five examples of how they did this:

- They were one of the first housing associations in the country to commit not to evict any of its residents due to a loss of income from the coronavirus, before legislation preventing evictions was announced.

- They kept residents informed through regular news updates on their website and weekly e-newsletters to those signed up for their digital services.

- For employees who were unable to do their usual jobs, they were empowered to volunteer with local charities to deliver food parcels to residents in need and make welfare calls to older and more vulnerable people living in their properties.

- They helped hundreds of residents apply for benefits and worked with partners in the police and local council to tackle issues such as the illegal disposing of waste and anti-social behavior.

- They provided residents with online courses through their "Learn for Free" program and held chat groups to help keep people connected and ease social isolation.

For their people

The pandemic presented huge challenges to PCH as their workforce was suddenly separated into three very different groups, with 30% initially being put on furlough, 48% working from home, and 14% being asked to continue to work on site in their communities. What this meant was that they needed to quickly find a way to connect and communicate with them all, getting information to them in the right way and at the right time.

Their solution was to develop a COVID-19 hub on their employee communications platform that they named "Jannet," since in Plymouth, people are called "Janners." The hub delivered daily updates on COVID-19, operational information on what was critical to know in order to get their work done, as well as a section where employees could post stories and photos to share their personal experiences.

To kick things off with the employee posts, Angie Scott, Head of Communications, shared what she called her "confessions" post, detailing her experiences of juggling working from home and homeschooling, leading by example to show that it was OK to show the human struggles you were dealing with. Another great example came from a surprising source - an employee by the name of Mark, who Scott described as a "big burly builder," who decided that every day he would share a video that included a daily thought. He named it "Thoughts from Mark's mound" as he filmed them on a grass bank just outside PCH's stores building where he picked up his stock early each morning.

The platform proved to be extremely successful, with a massive 87% readership. Scott explained: "Through our daily updates, our staff felt connected and well informed. They also had somewhere to instantly raise their fears and concerns – it was a great temperature check of staff mood and morale, plus a really good indicator of emerging issues. This meant all the difference in acting quickly and solving issues before they became problems. It helped to build valuable trust and confidence between our senior managers making important decisions and our workforce. We made absolutely sure we were living our values – we weren't just saying it, we listened, respected our staff's views and cared enough to take action. Most importantly we made sure we were doing the right things."

STUDENT MAIDS

The company

Student Maid is a Florida-based cleaning and concierge service dedicated to providing exceptional customer service while at the same time empowering the rising generation of leaders. When you hire from Student Maid, you are investing in opportunities for local students to learn and grow, taking these life skills, confidence in themselves, and leadership abilities as they approach their futures.

Their values

Student Maid's ten values are:

1.	Take your moral fiber	2.	Roll with the punches
3.	Jump through flaming hoops	4.	Don't leave us hangin'
5.	Be classy, not sassy	6.	Own it
7.	Unleash the creative dragon within	8.	Pay it forward
9.	Speak now or forever hold your peace	10.	Raise the roof

Bringing their values out to play

For their people

Student Maid used their values to react to and support their people throughout these challenging times. Whether it's through their value "**own it**," which is about taking ownership for your situation, accepting responsibility, and acting on it, or "***jump through flaming hoops***," which is about going above and beyond for each other, or "**roll with the punches**," which is about adapting to and accepting changes as it comes instead of resisting it, their values have come out to play countless times.

An example is when they made the decision to temporarily close their business well before they were mandated to do so by the state, not wanting to put their employees or customers at risk until they had adequate personal protection equipment (PPE) or cleaning products.

"We couldn't look at it from a revenue perspective; that would've meant we had to stay open, no matter what. Instead, we asked ourselves – if money were no object, what decision would we make? The answer was obvious, we had to close our business until we could ensure everyone's safety. We knew we would lose a ton in revenue, but to us, there was no other option we would accept," said Kristen Hadeed, CEO & founder.

But that left them with another dilemma, as closing the business meant their team members would no longer get the paychecks they relied on to pay for rent, tuition, groceries, and other bills. And since cutting them off from their livelihood didn't align with their value of "**don't leave us hangin'**," Student Maid made the decision to pay employees as much as they could for each pay period they were closed.

They crunched the numbers and found that they could give each member of the team $200 per paycheck, which for the majority of their part-time cleaners would be similar to what they would have made anyway, but for others, it wouldn't be nearly enough. So they called a virtual company-wide meeting, telling team members what they were able to do, giving employees who were going home to be with family the choice to give up part or all of the money to go to those who really needed it.

The response unequivocally confirmed their decision, with the team relieved that they didn't have to choose between a paycheck and their health, grateful that no one was being laid off and that the company was paying them what they could, while employees were able to step up to support one another.

The biggest impact of this and other actions has been the level of trust within their team, with employees seeing that when it mattered most, the company walked the talk and stuck to their values. "Long-term, we believe this translates to loyalty from our team members, and even our customers," said Hadeed.

TELEPERFORMANCE

The company

Teleperformance is the global leader in customer experience management, with over 300,000 interaction experts speaking 265 languages and dialects across 80 countries, serving over 170 markets.

Their values

Teleperformance's five values and the associated mantras are:

1. **Integrity:** "I do what I do, I do what I say."	2. **Respect:** "I treat others with kindness and empathy."
3. **Professionalism:** "I do things right the very first time."	4. **Innovation:** "I create and improve."
5. **Commitment:** "I am passionate and engaged."	

Bringing their values out to play

Teleperformance's (TP) mission and values represent how they think and act every day to achieve their main goal, "***happiness from inside out.***" And this was no different throughout the pandemic, with each of the five values shining through the actions taken by Teleperformance to support their community and employees.

For the community

TP employees have always been committed to supporting their

community, ranging from their "Knitters & Knatters Club," where they got together to knit hats for hospital neonatal units, to volunteering time at care homes to help with gardening, acting as reading buddies, and so much more. But with this no longer being possible, they pivoted to continue to provide support with different forms of kindness and empathy.

One way they did this was with their "Keep Smiling" campaign, which had the taglines of "working together to keep the nation smiling, helping care homes spread the joy." Cards were designed by TP employees and family members that displayed hand-drawn images and upbeat messages such as "Be strong, things will get better," "Storms don't last forever," and "Keep smiling." Uplifting messages were written on cards and sent to residents in care homes as well as key workers, delivering them along with treats so that they didn't feel forgotten and, of course, kept smiling.

For their people

And when it came to their people, TP again went above and beyond to provide support in this new world. "We started by asking our employees what they needed to keep them engaged, to stay healthy, and to stay connected," said Lisa Dolan, Head of Employee Engagement for UK & South Africa.

To help, TP created a number of channels to make sure they could connect with employees, keeping them up to date with important company news, and to share tips on how to look after themselves. One example was their "Keeping the kids busy" channel, where they shared crafting ideas, homeschooling tips, how to keep kids active, and even weekly activity packs for TP Tots and TP Teens. Another example was their "Your Health & Wellbeing" channel, where they shared tips and articles on how to keep the mind and body healthy, and links to activities such as Mindful 10:10, which were ten minute mindfulness sessions held at, you guessed it, 10:00 am.

TP also used competitions to drive connections throughout the pandemic, putting their creativity on display. These ranged from an Easter craft competition for kids, to a poetry competition for employees and family members where they could submit a poem about someone they looked up to as a hero, to a TelePETformance competition where photos were submitted showcasing the talents or funny habits of their pets. You name it, and they had a competition for it, all serving as a means to connect, interact, and celebrate together.

THE GRANITE GROUP

The company

The Granite Group (TGG) is a third generation family-owned U.S. distributor of plumbing, heating, cooling, water, and propane supplies. With 45 branches across six states in New England, including both wholesale and retail locations, the company prides themselves on providing best-in-class products and services to their customers. Their team of nearly 600 delivers on this by living up to the company's tagline of: "Solid as our name."

Their values

TGG's six values, which are held together through the acronym "Praise," are:

1. Professional	2. Relationships	3. Aggressive
4. Integrity	5. Service	6. Entrepreneurial

Bringing their values out to play

For the community

TGG has always been a community-focused organization, with their "TGG Cares" Committee organizing volunteering events for employees to participate in, and with the company providing financial support, reimbursing employees up to $250 for volunteering activities. But when the pandemic hit, and volunteering activities such as organized charity runs were no longer taking place, they decided to pivot and create a new way of giving back and, at the same time, do something to support the physical and mental health of their employees.

The result was an organized "Virtual 5k," where they invited employees to run or walk a 5k on their own, submitting pictures to celebrate and share their experiences with one another. And for every employee that participated, TGG donated $25 to their local food bank, giving back to the community in this much-needed way. This initiative showcases TGG values such as "**integrity**," doing the right thing for the community, and "**entrepreneurial**," finding ways to make things happen.

For their people

TGG has always had a strong culture, and, borrowing from their tag line, it was "as solid as their name." Their values and culture helped them stay strong throughout the pandemic, supporting and caring for their people so they could support and care for one another and for their customers.

One way was by keeping their workforce informed throughout the pandemic, doing so through a comprehensive and thorough communications strategy. Led by their executive virus response team that was put in place from day one, they sent out daily communications from CEO Bill Condron to provide updates, sharing both good news and bad. They also committed to answering employee questions within 15 minutes, and although they were fast and furious, the team managed to respond to them all. "We took a thoughtful approach to communications from the beginning, we met people where they were at, trying to approach everything with empathy, listening to their individual needs," said Tracie Sponenberg, Chief People Officer.

Another way was by pivoting and moving their annual employee meeting to a virtual event. Packed with information and business updates, the event helped add a bit of normality and at the same time, re-connect the entire workforce. "While it was tough not to see everyone in person, it was wonderful to see everyone online, from their homes," said Sponenberg. And to make it feel more like their annual meeting, each employee was sent a voucher for a free pizza.

TGG also lived their value of "**entrepreneurial**" in how they encouraged their individual locations to run their businesses throughout the pandemic. After receiving protocols on how to keep their people and customers safe, they were given the freedom to decide where to go from there. For example, did they want to open their doors for customers or have curb-side pickups? The choice was left up to individual owners to decide what was right for them.

The company

Tony's Chocolonely was founded in 2005 by journalists from the Dutch TV-program "Keuringsdienst van Waarde" (Food Unwrapped) after they discovered that the big chocolate manufacturers sourced cocoa from farms with illegal child labor. Since then, Tony's has grown to be the number one chocolate brand in the Netherlands, expanding into the U.S., UK and EU to deliver on their important mission and create an even bigger impact.

Their values

Tony's Chocoloney's four values are:

1. Outspoken	2. Makes you smile
3. Willfull	4. Entrepreneurial

Bringing their values out to play

For the community

The value of "**makes you smile,**" which talks about looking at the bright side, to keep laughing, and being full of energy to move chocolate mountains, was lived time and time again throughout the pandemic. In fact, it's meaning became even deeper, delivering smiles in different ways to support and reinforce their long term commitments to everyone they worked with.

Whether it was the people who came into the office to serve lunch, give chair massages or lead personal training classes to employees, or cocoa farmer partners in Africa, Tony's supported and put smiles on their faces throughout the pandemic in a variety of ways. They did it financially, paying them their normal fees regardless of whether the actual work was done, by staying connected to them, checking in to see how they were doing, or in the case of the farmers, helping them navigate through the situation together.

Here's a statement that talks about this last act of support from their website:

"For the cocoa farmers we work with, the coronavirus is a real threat. Keeping social distance is even harder if you live in a small house with your extended family and have no way to stock up on groceries for a week. Even simple extra hygienic measures are difficult when you rely on communal water points and soap is a luxury. By putting up posters with health precautions, as well as handing out leaflets and locally-made soaps, we promote and support preventive measures. In addition, we are also leveraging the network of community facilitators and Tony's ambassadors to raise awareness about the virus. Spread the word, not the virus!"

For their people

The value of "**makes you smile**" was also front and center in everything Tony's did to support their people throughout the pandemic. As Sophie Dopheide, Culture Champion, said, "We always try to make our team smile, especially in this surreal period!" Here are just two of the many ways they did this:

- **Gift boxes** - each week during lockdown, employees received special gift boxes. The first one was a QuaranTony survival kit, packed with the essentials required for lockdown including Red Bull and Jagermeister, since their company ski trip was cancelled due to the pandemic. Others included food from local restaurants, to put smiles on the faces of not only their employees, but also the businesses they were supporting. And to close out lockdown, the final box was a Staycation kit, packed with everything to have a beach holiday at home since travel was still not allowed, and on a more serious note, the choice of a few books on the topic of anti-racism.

- **Recognition wheel** - at Tony's, they have a "Wheel of Wonders" that employees can spin whenever they win the Tony's Award or other recognition awards. During the pandemic they adapted it to be the "QuaranTony Wheel," that employees could spin after winning one of their many online quizzes or other virtual team activities taking place during lockdown. Some of the wheel prizes were a six-pack of Corona, toilet paper, a voucher for a visit to the hairdressers, a LEGO kit, a movie night kit, and a voucher for a meal cooked by their office chef.

"In everything we did for our people during the pandemic, we wanted to bring our strong culture and rituals to their homes, creating connections and driving engagement," said Dopheide.

They did this by living another value, "entrepreneurial," which talks about pushing limits and breaking barriers to get things done. It's safe to say that Tony's accomplished this, proven by their creativity and perseverance to put smiles on the faces of their people and the wider community time and time again.

TWINKL

The company

Twinkl Educational Publishing began life in 2010 as a husband and wife start-up, working from a tiny back bedroom. Today, Twinkl is a truly global business, providing over half a million resources and content to support teachers and leaders around the world. Everything they do supports the global teaching community, being committed to transforming people's lives through education.

Their values

Twinkl's four values are:

1. Lead the way	2. Go above and beyond
3. Do the right thing	4. Be lovely

Bringing their values out to play

For the community

When schools began to close because of COVID-19, the Twinkl team recognized that through their mission to "**help those who teach**" and their value of "**do the right thing,**" they could and should be a part of the solution, supporting not just schools but parents, who for the first time had to become the teacher. So they quickly offered free access to their library of over 650,000 educational resources to both teachers and parents to keep their children learning at home.

They also lived the value of "**lead the way**" as they shifted priorities to what mattered most during the pandemic, redeploying their teams to make their home learning hub easier for parents in their new capacity of a teacher. "Parents are not trained to teach, so they look for and use resources in different ways. This meant we had to adapt our platform to meet their needs, creating a tool that was accessible and easy for them to use," said Tim Elgar, Head of Culture and Leadership. The updated hub now provides daily activities to help fill the days and offer much-needed variety, as well as book readings, live lessons, positive news updates, and more to help the overall learning experience.

The response has been extremely positive, with more and more people from across the world sending in messages about how much the resources have helped. And the same is true with their team members, with the experience uniting them behind their mission and values, making them proud to work for a company that has contributed throughout the crisis.

For their people

Twinkl recognized early on that in the same way that their learning hub delivers a flexible approach to learning, they needed to create and deliver a flexible approach to how their team members would work remotely. "The office environment is the same for everyone, but working at home differs drastically based on your personal circumstances. Some have kids at home with them, some live alone, others are in an apartment living with a group of friends. We wanted to tell team members that it was OK to do what's right for them," said Elgar.

So aligning with their value of "**be lovely,**" which talks about seeking to be helpful, being transparent, speaking up, and psychological safety, they created what they called their "It's OK" campaign. Each week messages were sent out that shared examples of what it was OK to do or feel. Some examples were that it's OK to have more catch-ups, talk about work-life balance, grab a virtual coffee, switch off your notifications at the end of the day, ignore devices during a break, tell someone you'll get back to them as soon as you can, change your working style to adapt to home working, and suggest ideas to help your team adapt.

These messages gave team members guidance so they didn't have to work out the unwritten rules for themselves, and so they understood what is expected and not expected of them. It helped them "**be lovely,**" based on what that was and meant to them personally, and "**do the right thing**" for themselves and for the company.

VAYNERMEDIA

The company

VaynerMedia is a global digital marketing agency that builds creative campaigns from insights gained through micro-content to produce and ultimately drive actual business results. They propel some of the biggest brands in the world to the intersection of attention and culture through their teams in New York, Los Angeles, London, and Singapore.

Their values

VaynerMedia's seven values, or what they call guiding principles, are:

1. Tenacious	2. Teamwork
3. Entrepreneurship	4. Empathy
5. Curiosity	6. Optimism
7. Gratitude	

Bringing their values out to play

For their people

Throughout the pandemic, VaynerMedia continued to live by their values, or as Claude Silver, Chief Heart Officer said, "Continue to walk our talk and do the right thing for our customers and our people."

One example is in how they treated employees being let go during the pandemic, which is no different than their pre-pandemic process, weaving the value "***empathy***" in from beginning to end.

"It's all about how you make someone feel in those moments when you are changing up their lives," said Silver. And for this reason, the team at VaynerMedia looked at each person individually, being proactive in understanding their needs and adapting their approach empathetically to suit them.

"It's about integrity in words and actions, understanding your impact, and landing in a way that doesn't crush the person but sets them up for the future," said Silver.

Another example is with their "12 at 12 sessions," which were born out of as Silver said, her "selfish desire to connect with my people." She offered these online sessions to anyone, and, you may have figured out, they happened at 12 every day.

These sessions combined fun activities such as icebreakers, as well as the opportunity for employees to honestly speak about how they were feeling and doing. "It was a great way to connect people from around the world who didn't know each other as well as those who worked in the same office who didn't know each other," said Silver.

They have been such a success that Gary Vaynerchuk, CEO, has started doing his own version of them as well. They complement the other ways that he has communicated throughout the pandemic, openly and transparently, living the company values to support the team through these challenging times.

VIISI

The company

Viisi is a company based in the Netherlands that specializes in mortgage advice. Their mission is to change their industry, making it more sustainable and more focused in the long term, doing so through their services and through their people-first principle and approach. This has worked well for them, with their business significantly growing over the years while achieving impressive customer ratings of 9.8 out of 10.

Their values

At Viisi they chose not to have a "standard" list of values, instead they have what they call their "***Golden Rule.***" As Tom van der Lubbe, Co-Founder said, "You can find the Golden Rule in most religions. It says you should treat others like you want to be treated yourself. The rest is common sense—there are no other rules."

Bringing their values out to play

For their people

At Viisi, putting their people first and living their Golden Rule have helped them be voted "Best Workplace" since 2016, winning first place in 2019 and 2020. So as they entered the pandemic and faced the challenges faced by most organizations, it was only natural for them to be front and center in how they made business and people decisions.

One example has been in their approach to layoffs. As van der Lubbe explained in his blog titled "It's About Solidarity, Stupid! (Why Avoiding

Layoffs Makes Sense)":

"It's all about your people. Now more than ever. But in knee-jerk reactions to the coronavirus many companies are laying off large numbers. I want to shout out to the shareholder-value managers driven by their spread-sheets: This is not only inhumane. It is bad for your business! Why? It will harm your company. Companies that treat their people best in bad times emerged as winners in the past."

And with this mindset, Viisi managed to avoid layoffs throughout the crisis so far.

Another example is in how they decided to treat and support their employees as they went into lockdown and had to deal with their individual challenges. They came up with three categories of employees that were based on their personal work and home circumstances, **paying them their full salary regardless of the category**:

1. **Green:** These employees could and did work their normal hours.

2. **Orange**: These employees could work part-time as they had parenting, homeschooling or other responsibilities for the remainder.

3. **Red:** These employees could choose not to work at all as they had a partner who was a key worker, or a family member who tested positive for coronavirus.

The idea behind this approach was to support the entire person, both from a work and a home perspective. It was also about supporting one another, showing their strong solidarity as a team, working together to get the work done. As van der Lubbe said, "It's about having those with strong shoulders help to carry and support the others."

Both of these examples really brought to life the concept of the Golden Rule, deviating from the norm to focus on doing what's right, regardless of the short-term cost. And what about the cost to the business? Well, according to van der Lubbe, "we had higher productivity throughout because we removed employee's fears and created psychological safety. At the end, it's just a human thing: We treated each other as human beings and not as human resources."

WELCOME BREAK

The company

Welcome Break is one of the UK's leading independent motorway service operators, having 27 sites spread across the country that are open 24 hours a day, 365 days a year and attracts 85 million motorway customers annually. Their purpose is to delight road-weary travellers by offering unexpectedly human experiences in comfortable, clean, and safe surroundings, aiming to make people feel human again, energized and ready for their journey ahead.

Their values

Welcome Break's three values are:

1. We care	2. We are a team	3. We deliver

Bringing their values out to play

For their people

Welcome Break found themselves in a challenging situation as the UK went into lockdown. They had to balance the needs of their 3,500 employees who were being put on furlough, and because the government required them to remain open and provide essential services, the 1,500 who needed to come to work at their motorway service stations.

They rose to the challenge fueled by their value "**we care,**" doing so in a variety of big and little ways, taking the concept of care to the next level. Here are just a few of them:

- **Food allowance** - prior to the pandemic, only managers received a food allowance to pay for their meals when they worked at one of their motorway service stations. But to show they cared about every employee coming into work during lockdown, they extended it to them all. "We wanted everyone to have a lunch on us" said Nicola Marshall, People Director.

- **Isolation hotline** - when the symptoms of COVID-19 first came out, Welcome Break quickly decided to set up an isolation hotline, somewhere employees could go for timely and accurate information on this very confusing and critical topic. They pulled two members of the HR team to work on this, asking them to read every piece of government guidance to ensure they were equipped to support the over 500 employees who at some point in time needed to go into isolation.

  They had one person who dealt with employee queries, and the other who called each person in isolation personally to understand their symptoms and give them guidance. In addition, they created a 30-page FAQ document that was posted on their intranet that included the most up-to-date information and links, requiring the team to keep on top of the changes happening nearly every day.

- **Clap for the team** - to thank their employees for their contributions during lockdown, the team at Welcome Break created their own version of the UK Thursday night clap for the NHS celebration. They created a short video that included each member of the leadership team saying thank you as they clapped, with the overall message being "tonight we clap for you."

- **Coloring competition** - they held a coloring competition for the children of their employees, asking them to create a poster about the topic of washing your hands. The winner had their image hung up in the restrooms, showing they cared for each other by understanding and respecting this important and essential practice.

- **Leadership pay cut** - and finally, to show that they cared and also to live the value of "*we are a team*," the leadership team took a 20% pay cut. This showed that it was not just furloughed employees who were having their salaries reduced by 20% (the UK government furlough scheme paid 80% of their salary), but that the leaders would make a sacrifice to show that they were in it together.

The company

YMCA St Paul's Group (YMCA) is a charity that works across London and beyond to support young people and communities. They do this by providing services to vulnerable and homeless young people, working with children, youth and families in the community, running five Health and Wellbeing Centers, and offering a range of inclusive activities to meet local needs and provide a safe space to learn new skills, get healthier, meet people, and make a connection.

Their values

The YMCA's four values are:

1. Inclusive	2. Aspirational
3. Excellent	4. Honest

Bringing their values out to play

For the community

The safety and wellbeing of their young people and their communities are at the heart of what the YMCA does, delivering on their vision of "helping young people and communities thrive and flourish." This did not change during the pandemic, although they had to find new ways to deliver these critical services and this level of support in different ways.

Here are a few ways they did this:

- **Virtual gym classes** - as their gyms were being closed, the

YMCA very quickly responded by moving to virtual gym classes, offering them not only to their members, but to anyone for free with a voluntary donation.

- **Virtual choir** - with donations received, they set up a virtual choir as a way to help the elderly with feelings of isolation. Whether they were a part of the choir or just listened, it was a way to be a part of something and feel connected to others.

- **Support to youth** - to ensure that the youth continued to feel supported and engaged during these very challenging times, they moved activities and resources online. And since many did not have access to technology, through funding received, they provided free smartphones and tablets, ensuring they could easily access these critical tools, networks and resources.

- **Counselling to residents** - for residents in their hostels, they quickly realized that they needed a different kind of support, so quickly adapted what and how they delivered counselling. They focused on making sure that everyone understood lockdown rules, that they felt safe and that they did not feel alone.

For their people

The wellbeing of their employees was also a focus of the YMCA during the pandemic, placing their people first, which aligns with their value of being "*inclusive.*"

Here are a few ways they did this:

- **Coffee mornings** - they held virtual coffee mornings with employees as a way to provide updates from the leadership team and to help everyone continue to feel engaged and connected.

- **Appreciation video** - to thank their frontline heroes, they created a number of special appreciation videos that contained words of appreciation from colleagues and managers, sharing via WhatsApp and the organization's intranet with their workforce and the wider YMCA community.

- **Supported working from home** - when they moved to remote working, the YMCA very quickly made the decision to make sure that everyone was equipped to effectively work from home. One example was by paying for internet service for those that previously did not have it, and sending chairs and screens to people's homes to ensure that they could do their job and stay connected in this new virtual world.

- **Supported work-life balance -** to encourage and support employees taking the time to get the balance right between home and work, they came up with a variety of initiatives that were driven by their CEO. One was putting an hour each day in calendars for breaks, having a no meeting day booked in each week, having end of week virtual cocktail evenings and pub quizzes as well as sharing videos of what they'd done in their time off to get people talking. All of this was designed to help people talk about the important parts of wellbeing.

- **New engagement hub** - during lockdown, the YMCA launched "Thrive," their new online one-stop-shop employee engagement hub as a way to help employees feel connected, to support their wellbeing, and to drive employee recognition. "We launched during COVID as a way to unify the organization, putting in place tools and resources to help our people and stay connected whether they were onsite working or on furlough," said Nicola Kent, Head of Organizational Development.

ZIP CO LIMITED

The company

Zip Co Limited (Zip) offers point-of-sale credit and digital payment services to consumers and merchants in Australia, NZ, U.S. and the UK. Their driven team of "Zipsters" is passionate about providing alternative digital payment and credit solutions that make people's lives easier, giving them greater freedom and control.

Their values

Zip's four values are:

1. Customer first	2. Own it
3. Stronger together	4. Change the game

Bringing their values out to play

For the community

Throughout the pandemic, Zip was responsive to the changing needs of their customers, living their "**customer first**" value in a variety of ways. Here are a few ways that Zip continued to put the customer first:

- Ensured customers were aware of their hardship policy, helping them work through loan repayments to meet their financial needs and challenges.

- Fast-tracked the development of a new product called "Shop Everywhere," which allowed their customers to use their Zip app to pay interest-free online for products at almost every online retailer.

- Let customers know they could pay household bills by using their Zip account, allowing them to settle bills with the provider right away, but paying it off over time, interest-free.

- Shared with customers that other essentials such as fuel and groceries could be purchased with the clever use of pre-purchased Zip gift cards.

- Supported merchant partners who were struggling with a loss of in-store traffic by helping them to move to online shopping, introducing them to a new customer base.

By understanding the impact of the pandemic on their customers, and then adapting their products and services accordingly, Zip was able to help customers control their finances during these unprecedented times. As Larry Diamond, CEO and co-founder, said, "We're living through one of the toughest challenges of our generation. We've never known a situation like this. More than ever, we need to be there for each other."

For their people

Zip was also responsive to the needs of their people, their other customers, showing this in numerous ways, such as:

- **Mental health support** - as in other organizations, employees at Zip were dealing with an extra level of anxiety and stress due to the pandemic. Because of this, they encouraged employees to take time off if they felt it was necessary, paying them their regular salary. "We didn't want our employees to have their finances as another stress trigger, having to decide between taking time off to focus on their mental wellbeing or paying their bills," said Jennifer Mumford, Director of People & Development. One of the ways they did this was through a "Zip Day Off" over a long weekend to give their team extra time to recover, spend time with loved ones and say "thank you."

- **"Meet the executives"** - at the start of the pandemic, the team moved to weekly All Hands virtual meetings, incorporating a new "meet the executive" section. Executives shared pictures from their childhoods, including awkward teenage photos, and told stories of pivotal moments in their lives that made them who they were today. "It showed the human side of our executives, showing vulnerability, sharing stories and acting in a way to bring the team closer together despite everything else going on in the world," said Mumford.

- **Supporting managers** - at Zip, a lot of first time managers were asked to step up and lead in a different way, due to lockdown. To support them, the team ran focus groups to gauge feedback, discover pain points and just understand day-to-day emotions. On the back of this, they introduced virtual Zip Lead and global leadership communities, connecting leaders to share their experiences and lessons along the way. One fun part of this was introducing 1:1s with emojis to kick off conversations about how people were doing during these unprecedented times.

ZOOM

The company

Zoom is a global company that helps businesses and individuals bring teams, family, and friends together in an easy, reliable, and frictionless cloud platform. Committed to delivering happiness, believing that the greatest, most sustainable happiness comes from making others happy, they deliver this through their platform every single day.

Their values

Zoom's five values, which all center around the concept of "care," are:

1. We care for community	2. We care for customers
3. We care for company	4. We care for teammates
5. We care for ourselves	

Bringing their values out to play

As Zoom's business exploded almost overnight, expanding from a B2B (business-to-business) to a B2C (business-to-consumer) company, they worked around the clock to innovate and make sure their product was frictionless and supported the needs of their existing and new customers. From grandmas to six-year-olds, from CEOs to Prime Ministers, their product showed every customer that Zoom cared about them, and at the same time, allowed customers to show they cared for others.

"Knowing the difference our platform was making was the glue that held the Zoom team together as they worked tirelessly to overcome challenges such as privacy and security in this new world. We shared stories that brought to life our culture of caring and our mission to deliver happiness," said Lynne Oldham, Chief People Officer.

For the community

At the start of the pandemic, Zoom decided to adjust the product to support new use cases. One key group for this product were teachers, who when schools abruptly closed in the middle of the school year, were faced with the challenge of teaching students who were now based at home. So they reached out to schools to give them free access to their platform, resulting in more than 100,000 schools in 25 countries using Zoom as their virtual classrooms.

Another way Zoom supported the community was by partnering with the American Heart Association (AHA) for the "**#TakeABreak**" initiative, aimed at encouraging people to set personal boundaries as the lines blurred between work and home. They worked together to create programs that encouraged people to set personal boundaries, putting their health first and giving them time to disconnect.

"I'm happy to be rolling out this program with the AHA," said Zoom founder and CEO Eric S. Yuan. "While Zoom has been helping people stay connected and productive during this pandemic, we know that never unplugging can cause stress and affect heart health. I deeply value happiness and mental health and have been personally impacted by cardiovascular disease in a family member. I want our company to lead the way in empowering people to put their health first." For their people Zoom also showed their people that they cared, delivering happiness in many ways. With the help of their employee-run Happy Crew, they sent out care packages and held numerous Zoom-related virtual activities such as an open mic night, meditation and fitness classes. Two additional examples of caring, the first sponsored by the Women's Employee Resource Group (ERG) and the second by the People Experience team, are:

For their people

Zoom also showed their people that they cared, delivering happiness in many ways. With the help of their employee-run Happy Crew, they sent out care packages and held numerous Zoom-related virtual activities such as an open mic night, meditation and fitness classes. Two additional examples of caring, the first sponsored by the Women's Employee Resource Group (ERG) and the second by the People Experience team, are:

- **Camp Zoomitude** - since many employees didn't have somewhere to go for the summer because of the pandemic, they took the idea of Zoomitude, which is their word for "gratitude," and created Camp Zoomitude, bringing summer camp in-house. Both kids and parents loved that three days a week they could join in on camp-based activities as well as the Friday recap called "Smores N More" with a family sing-a-long where they were joined by the CEO himself!

- **Wellbeing** - wellbeing was a key focus throughout the pandemic, with Zoom stepping up to support people as they dealt with the challenges of the times, making it more accessible and meaningful to their workforce. One way was by changing the monthly wellness payment, letting employees use it in any way they felt best supported their individual needs. From using it for food delivery to buying things for their home office to home exercise equipment, it helped employees get through the crisis with the support of Zoom.

Conclusion

Let me end by wishing you all the best on your values journey. I hope your values will play an active and important role in helping to fuel you and your people to new and wonderful destinations.

Remember to challenge and push yourself to have *the best* values, and don't settle for anything less. And then, put tons and tons of effort into bringing them out to play time after time, again by challenging and pushing yourself to do it in a truly effective way. I've shared tons of tips and plays on how to do this throughout the book, so please draw assistance and inspiration from them, and then go out there and do it in your own unique and special way.

And speaking of doing things in your own way, I couldn't end the book without sharing with you my values, the ones I discovered and bring out to play at my new company, DebCo HR. They are to the point, straightforward and a bit unique – just like me and my work. They motivate and keep me true to my mission, and, at the same time, show my clients and potential clients what they can expect when working with me.

I'm quite proud of this logo for it not only shares my two values, but thanks to the wonderful designer, Joy Adan, the design itself brings further meaning to what the values stand for. Here are the meanings behind her brilliant designs, and what some of the letters stand for:

Open the door to possibilities

- O = the compass indicates leading and helping others using knowledge and experience.

- P = the brain indicates rebelliously presenting new ideas and ways of thinking.

- N = the arrow pointing up indicates a positive, optimistic and can-do attitude.

Create magic

- R = the star indicates magic and sparkle put into the work.

- E = the speech bubble indicates conversation and connection taking place.

- A = the lightbulb indicates ideas that get to the heart of what others need to do to resolve their challenges and situations.

- T = the hammer shows the hard work going into building solutions.

- E = the rocket indicates reaching for the stars and exploring uncharted territory to deliver the best experience and solutions.

By putting this extra layer of meaning into my values, it makes them that much better and that much clearer for me and for my audience. Did it take more time and work to do this? Yes, but it was worth it in the end. Which leads me nicely into my final words, which are to keep in mind that at times your values journey may be a struggle, it may seem like an uphill battle, but it will be worth it in the end. As the talented musician, Miles Davis said, "Sometimes you have to play a long time to play like yourself." So, go out there and play with your values and help your company and people be who they are and need to be!

Acknowledgements

This book has been a true collaborative effort, and for that, I am most grateful. Whether you helped me directly by agreeing to be interviewed, or indirectly by inspiring me through the books you wrote, let me thank you for helping me create a rich and diverse collection of thoughts, tips and stories. I learned so much writing the book, and I'm confident that all those who read it will as well.

Let me start out by thanking my 'playwrights', those of you who were kind enough to let me interview you and share your wonderful stories (plays) for the book. Here they are in alphabetical order: Mat Davies from Addison Lee Group, Dominic Price and Bek Chee from Atlassian, Már Másson from Blue Lagoon Iceland, Andrew Constable from Brown Forman, Phil Burgess from C Space, Sarah Mortimer from Charles Tyrwhitt, Tracey Lake and Sue Lowe from Credit Union Australia, Nataliya Wilson from DaVita, Pierre David from Decathlon, Breckon Jones from Deloitte Australia, Andrew O'Callaghan from Dishoom, Misty Johnson Oratokhai and Lashell Mindingall from Events DC, Alastair Gill from giffgaff, Mathew Paine from ICC Sydney, Henrik Stenmann and Caroline Tindborg from IIH Nordics, Anna Pearson from Impraise, Lawrence Cramer and Jamie Bunce from Inspired Villages, Martin Green from KidZania London, Johanna Dickinson from KP Snacks, Troels Wendelbo and Eunice Clements-Tweedie from LEGO Group, Tara Barley and Glenn Grayson from Missguided, Lyvia Nabarro from MOSL, Marcus Lamont and Fiona Furman from NAHL Group plc, Levi King from Nav, Bethany Mullett from Otsuka, Maree Morgan-Monk and Danica Vujik from Peoplecare, Nikki Gatenby from Propellernet,

Calum Macrae from Purina, Amy Bastuga from Radio Flyer, Katy Grêlé from Ralph Trustees, Robert Hicks from Reward Gateway, Steve Foster from St John Ambulance, Lars van Wieren from Starred, Sharon Ashcroft from TrustFord, Brian McCarthy from Valor Hospitality, Paul Venables from Venables Bells + Partners, Suzanne Roddie from Virgin Atlantic, Garry Ridge and Rachelle Snook from WD-40 Company, , and Maritza Lewis from Zappos.

Let me next thank the authors of those books that I used for my research. If you don't have their books on your reading list, I'd suggest doing so, as they're all great in different ways. Here they are in alphabetical order:

1. *Built it: The Rebel Playbook for Employee Engaged* by Glenn Elliott and me
2. *Built to Last* by Jim Collins and Jerry Porras
3. *Dare to Lead* by Brené Brown
4. *Delivering Happiness* by Tony Hsieh
5. *Engaged!* by Gregg Lederman
6. *Great Mondays* by Josh Levine
7. *Helping People Win at Work* by Ken Blanchard and Garry Ridge
8. *Leaders Eat Last* by Simon Sinek
9. *People with Purpose* by Kevin Murray
10. *Powerful* by Patty McCord
11. *Start with Why: How Great Leaders Inspire Everyone to Take Action* by Simon Sinek
12. *Superengaged* by Nikki Gatenby
13. *Will it Make the Boat Go Faster?* by Harriet Beveridge and Ben Hunt-Davis

Next, I'd like to send my heartfelt thanks to Glenn Elliott, who pushed me to be a rebel when we wrote our last book together, and gave me gentle nudges with this book as well. The world would be a different place without special people like you!

And finally, I'd like to thank my amazing family: Ken, Chloe and Anthony, for being so patient and supportive throughout the writing process. They not only listened as I shared yet another story (play) with them, but they actually acted interested. I couldn't have done it without your encouragement and patience – I love you all!!